Paul Hill, contributing editor

Up the Creek With a Paddle

Building Effective Youth and Family Ministry

Augsburg Fortress

MINNEAPOLIS

Up the Creek WITH a Paddle: Building Effective Youth and Family Ministry

Cover and interior design: David Meyer
Cover photo: Sandy May Photography

ISBN 0-8066-3703-X

Manufactured in U.S.A.

2 3 4 5 6 7 8 9 0 1 2 3 4 5 6 7 8 9

In memory of Cynthia Quere Camphouse
and in honor of the
Quere and Camphouse families,
whose faith, courage, and love
are inspirational to us all.

How to Use This Book or
READ THIS PAGE FIRST!

Those who labor in youth and family ministry are like canoeists going upstream. We paddle and pull each day against the currents of the culture, competitive forces, and parents who expect US to turn their children into faithful Christians. Our metaphorical arms burn, backs ache, and energy drops as we paddle on. Sometimes it feels like we are getting nowhere. I once was paddling in such a situation and noted to my bowman that the stump on shore already had passed us three times; the only thing worse would be if we didn't have paddles!

Paddles are critical for canoeists. If a paddle breaks, then all control is lost and one tumbles down the river, following the whims of the current. Paddles give control. Paddles, and knowing how to use them, help us move ahead—and in the right direction. This book is about paddles: twenty-one paddles that will keep you going in the direction you want to go in youth and family ministry. Apply these paddles to navigate the waters, and watch yourself move closer and closer to your destination. You'll leave the stumps in your wake.

The point is that youth and family ministry is sometimes difficult, counter-cultural, often tiring work. All evangelism is like that. (See Proverb 1 for details.) Because of the nature of the work, we even toyed with titling this book "Salmon Aren't the Only Ones Swimming Upstream," but the metaphor broke down when we realized that the life of a salmon entails swimming like crazy against harsh currents in order to lay some seeds…and then die. Not exactly the word of hope you need to hear, right?

Good, strong paddles, however, help canoeists on many journeys over many rivers. They help to get us to those times when the wind is at our backs and the sun shines warm on our tan bodies, the struggles of the current forgotten in the joy of the experience.

Whether your youth and family ministry is a continual paddle upstream or a sail with the wind, this book is for you. You will gain three things from reading it:

1. You will grow in confidence as you develop wisdom in this ministry.

2. You will gain expertise in practical ways to navigate the waters of this ministry effectively.

3. You will develop a solid theological and philosophical base upon which you can do this ministry.

Not bad, huh? The real question is, Do people really read books from cover to cover? Authors would hope so, readers promise to…both live in denial. Therefore, we want to give you permission, right at the beginning, to not read this entire book. Feel better already, don't you? Having set your guilt aside, please DO READ THE REST OF THIS PAGE!

Think of this book as proverbs of wisdom (verbal paddles). It is the wise perspective of wise people who have done a lot of youth and family ministry over the years. Think of us as your canoe guides.

Knowing full well that you will pick and choose your proverbs of wisdom as needs arise, we have only one request: READ THE PREFACE AND INTRODUCTION or you will always paddle poorly against the current. They are that important.

We will know if you have done what we have asked, for an exploding paint ball is hidden within these pages. Should the secret timer not record that a suitable amount of time was spent on the preface and introduction, the paint ball will explode and cover you in salmon-pink paint. It takes a year to wash off. Your friends will stare and say, "Tried to skip the preface and introduction in the new youth and family ministry book, didn't you?" and your shame will be visible to all.

When you do read the preface and introduction, you will then understand the importance of the Four Keys as a tool for all youth and family ministry. You also will understand the central premise of our proverbs: Youth ministry that does not include parents and other caring adults is better called "canoeing over the falls." Can we all agree that this is to be avoided? Good!

You now have permission to begin your journey.

Paul Hill
Center for Youth Ministries of Wartburg Seminary
CYM@Ecunet.org

Table of Contents

Cross: Theological perspectives
Guitar: Cultural issues
Heads: Community and relationship issues
For further explanation of icons see page 11.

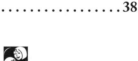

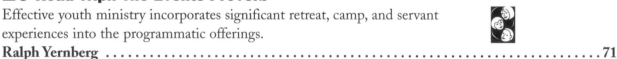

THE PRIMACY OF FAMILY PREFACE

Families. The family unit, however it is shaped, is the primary socialization and education force in the life of youth. The family is the single most effective means by which the faith is shared and appropriated by the next generation. Ministry with youth means ministry with the family.

When speaking about youth ministry, people in the church begin with a host of images and perceptions based on diverse experiences, assumptions, and desired goals. There are also varying understandings of youth and their needs. Before we speak of youth and family ministry as some kind of specialty, however, we need to get behind those established images and perceptions to the church's basic mission—people, faith, and life.

Loren Mead, one of the great advocates of the importance of congregations in fulfilling the mandate of the church, states: "It is my conviction that religious congregations are the most important carriers of meaning that we have, with one exception."[1] Mead notes that the one exception is the family. The vital source of meaning and purpose that he does not explore in his writings is family life, because it is not his expertise. Instead he wants to help church leaders develop what he believes is the second most important social entity, the Christian congregation.

Loren Mead may be able to direct his attention away from the family, but that does not give us in the church the privilege of ignoring this basic building block of life that has such an impact on individual lives and, therefore, congregations and the church at large. If we wish to explore that element of congregational life identified as youth ministry, then we dare not neglect that single most important ingredient in the lives of youth—their families. We cannot overlook the family as the vital transmitter of meaning, purpose, direction, values, and, yes, even faith, for our youth.

To put it simply, when we are speaking of Christian families, we are speaking of the church, for the Christian home is also the church. It is a gathering of believers who live their lives, empowered by the Holy Spirit for faith working through love (Galatians 5:6). There are those who question such a statement because of our current awareness that families are often exhausted and sometimes very unloving in their behavior. It is even suggested that our families are not capable of being vital partners in ministry because too many are in chaos.

However, the good news of Jesus Christ makes it clear that God works even through that which is sinful, broken, and dying: God works through broken vessels (2 Corinthians 4:7-12); God can use evil for good (Genesis 50:20); Christ died for the ungodly (Romans 5:6). If that were not so, not only would we give up on our families, we also would give up on our congregations.

Congregations, too, experience chaos, frustration, exhaustion, and even brutality. Like families, congregations can become dysfunctional units where sin dwells, but that need not and must not deter people of faith whose hope and love is in Christ Jesus. What better place to look than the family for an example of a community that embodies the ministry of reconciliation (2 Corinthians 5:19-20).

There is ample evidence that families have much to offer our congregational ministry with youth. The Scriptures assume that the home, composed of a variety of blood kin and other social relationships, is the primary location out of which the faith is passed on from generation to generation (see Exodus 10:2; Deuteronomy 6:7, 20-24; 11:1-3; Joshua 4:6-7; Acts 2:46-47; 16:29-34; Ephesians 6:1-4). Martin Luther wrote the Small Catechism for use in the home. He described parents as apostles, bishops, and priests to their children. His own family was a model of Christian living that included hospitality to guests, worship, singing, storytelling, Christian education, and conversation, all of which are expressions of the sharing of God's grace between the generations. Parents today remain the primary teachers of faith and values to their children. To ignore parents is to ignore God-given ministers of the gospel. Modern research confirms these biblical and historical convictions regarding the role of family (see the introduction).

A fundamental challenge to family-sensitive youth ministry is that we are not very confident of our ability to define family in a way that is inclusive. The fear is that when we speak of family, we will leave some people out, people who do not have a family—or at least the type of family to which some refer. The term *family* can easily divide people into political, religious, and sociological camps. Some people fear limiting family to mean the mother, father, children grouping that may not do justice to biblical or contemporary family diversity. Others fear the undermining of family life in general. For youth ministry to have its most enduring impact, the church needs to face these concerns and affirm the importance of a rich variety of families in the lives of youth.

Richard P. Olson and Joe H. Leonard Jr. offer a definition of family that can help lead estranged camps toward constructive conversation. They define the family as "any network of two or more people linked over time emotionally and usually biologically and/or legally, sharing such things as home, spiritual and material resources, interpersonal caregiving, memory, common agenda, and aspirations."[2]

Olson and Leonard offer a family systems approach to defining the nature and dynamics of families. This perspective recognizes that individuals are never self-defined entities (see Proverb 3). People are understood in the context of human relationships, especially the primary relationships that affect them on a regular basis. Their definition does not attempt to dictate a certain norm for the family unit that shapes the individuals within the family. Olson and Leonard refer to 40 types of family life that are mentioned or alluded to in the Bible. They conclude that "there was much more diversity in families than one might think. There is also as much family diversity in the Bible as there is in contemporary culture."[3] With this biblical perspective in mind, they and others recommend that we speak of "families" rather than "the family." The point is to acknowledge a galaxy of family constellations rather than one preferred model to impose on all others.

Effective youth ministry in the '90s and beyond is necessarily bound to family ministry. It welcomes the rich diversity of homes from which our youth come. Youth and family ministry works with youth from birth—or even prebirth—on. It seeks to have an impact on the homes of youth where parents or other caregivers are not necessarily interested in Christianity or the church. It finds nonthreatening ways to reach into those homes in order to nurture healthy family relations and help households consider the values, meaning, and hope that will lead them into a salutary and faith-filled future. Youth and family ministry reaches out to the unchurched youth through Christian homes that represent the front line of a congregation's evangelism into the community. For example, having youth invited into the homes of Christian youth and families to experience hospitality that includes a meal and table grace can be an effective means of outreach. It addresses daily-life issues and creates opportunities for intergenerational households to consider the importance of the spiritual life of the home.

Youth and family ministry is concerned about the lives of people and the faith that can give them abundant life (John 10:10). It is evident from research, daily-life experience, and the chronicles of the church that there are at least four keys that can nurture healthy relationships and faith at the same time. Those keys are as follows:

1. Caring conversation

2. Family rituals and traditions

3. A family devotional life

4. Intergenerational service to others that conveys the beliefs, values, and lifestyle of the home

These Four Keys become new wine that needs the new wineskin of a youth and family ministry in the congregation. In developing each proverb's discussion, the writers have taken these Four Keys seriously. They will guide you to effective practical steps. The new wineskin is a ministry built upon a partnership between home and congregation. The new wineskin of a youth and family ministry seeks a multitude of ways to announce the gospel to all ages and in a variety of settings, to edify individuals and households with evangelical care, and to exhort one another in Christian discipleship.

This book identifies key proverbs—wise maxims—for effective youth and family ministry. These proverbs can be applied to family settings as well as congregational and community settings. I applaud this broad-based, family-friendly approach to such a critical issue. Though written from their own perspectives, the authors share a common wisdom in their approaches that points us all to effective outreach to and with the young.[4]

David Anderson
Youth and Family Institute of Augsburg College

Thus, the Relationship Proverb (I Really Love You, Friend!) joins the Gospel and Family Proverbs as being the most critical, but without the others they flounder for lack of support. They cannot stand alone. However, if you are forced to prioritize where you plan to spend your time and energy in youth and family ministry, we believe you should focus on sharing the gospel, supporting families, and working to build Christian relationships with youth. Resources that emphasize these aspects are to be used.

In using this book to evaluate what you are currently doing in your congregation, ask first where in your current youth and family ministries you already give expression to these proverbs. The chart described in Appendix A will be helpful as you try to identify your strengths and growing edges as they relate to each of the proverbs.

Finally, you'll find that the book is written in such a way that each of the proverbs can stand on its own. Feeling comfortable in one area, you can move into another. The book is written in this way so that you can use it as an ongoing reference resource.

Few congregations or youth and family ministries have incorporated all 21 proverbs into their ministries. One need not worry about that. There is always room to grow. People who use compasses rarely get to the North Pole, but they do know where they are heading. That's the way in which this book can be used. All of us who have contributed to the book wish all of God's rich blessings to you and the youth and families with whom you work.

As contributing editor of this opus I extend my thanks and appreciation to all our writers: David Anderson, Kelly Chatman, Norma Cook Everist, Lyle M. Griner, Anne Helmke, Janet Lepp, Anne Marie Nuechterlein, Winston Persaud, Elizabeth Polanzke, JoAnn Post, Ralph Quere, Mike Rinehart, Thomas Schattauer, Susan Sherwood, and Ralph Yernberg. What a wonderful, crazy, insightful, fun group!

My thanks goes to Jean Rieniets, who, as office administrator, has shared the vision of the Center for Youth Ministries with me since the first day.

A special thanks to Elizabeth Polanzke, who, as our student assistant and a contributing author, brought much order to the process of organizing this book.

The late-night efforts of typist Valerie Way are also appreciated.

I wish to acknowledge the support of the people of Wartburg Theological Seminary, its board of directors, the faculty, and especially President Roger Fjeld, whose focus on mission inspires us all.

Finally, I extend my love and appreciation to my wife, Elaine, and my children, Josh and Amber. They are my most honest and helpful critics and my most ardent supporters.

Paul Hill

1
First Things First
The Gospel Proverb

by Paul Hill

> The gospel of Jesus Christ is the person, power, and purpose for Christian ministry with youth and families.

Go therefore and make disciples of all nations.
Matthew 28:19

Whatever!
Generation Next

Before you read any further in this book, answer this question: What is the primary purpose of the church? Don't cheat! Take some time and reflect.

Having thought about that question, now answer a second: What is the primary purpose of youth and family ministry?

In working with congregations and adults who work with youth, I like to start by asking these two questions of the group. The answers I receive vary considerably. Here are some sample responses to the question, What is the primary purpose of youth and family ministry?

■ To have kids attend the program.
■ To make sure our church has a future.
■ To keep the kids out of trouble.
■ Church is the only place that can address the terrible problems we have with our youth today.
■ To give the kids morals and values.
■ To provide hospitality and a safe place where kids can be kids.

In a sense all of the above answers are correct. And they all miss the mark. They all lift up valuable goals. None are primary.

The primary purpose of youth and family ministry is to be tools of the Holy Spirit in faith formation. We want to help our youth grow up believing in the person (God as a human being, manifested in Jesus); power (God defeats sin and death and restores life through Jesus' death and resurrection); and purpose (Jesus' believers are called to discern and do his will) of Jesus Christ. The essence of youth ministry is evangelism. Those who work with youth are evangelists and missionaries.

I can hear your thought process. "Whoa, Paul…EVANGELISM! MISSIONARIES! Those are old, out-of-date words. This sounds like you are trying to shove something down the kids' throats." This is an understandable reaction. Many Christians in our pluralistic society are squeamish when it comes to proselytizing. Many of us just can't help it—we are missionally shy.

Good excuses and explanations, to be sure, but the fact remains that youth and family ministry is primarily a work of evangelism. Our children don't spring from the womb reciting the Small Catechism; it must be taught. Our children are not born with a "Christian chromosome" that predetermines they will believe in God; God is experienced through the Holy Spirit. Our children do not automatically gravitate to a life in Christian community; they must be invited. Our children do not voluntarily sacrifice all to be disciples; they must see the work of God's kingdom in the efforts of the adults around them.

Many years ago, when I was a young adult, I was blessed with the opportunity to work at one of our Christian camps in the Boundary Waters Canoe Area of northern Minnesota. It was life shaping. One summer two members of the camp staff were getting married. They decided to tie the knot at the canoe base. Families, friends, and relatives converged on the camp and the festivities began. The sense of community, joy, sharing, and love was tremendous. Just prior to the wedding, one of the staff and I were walking on a camp trail with the bride's parents. Her father remarked, "This place is incredible. You people work so hard and care so much. What makes Wilderness Canoe Base so special?" Without missing a beat, my fellow staff member chirped, "Jesus Christ!" I'll never forget that moment. My peer had been nurtured and trained to know what was the primary focus of this entire camp ministry.

Youth can receive hospitality walking into Wal-Mart. Youth can find safe places in shelters, school clubs, YM/WCAs, synagogues, mosques, and city recreation centers. Youth can learn moral values in 4-H, Boy Scouts and Girl Scouts, sports teams, hobby groups, and more. However, only in the context of the Christian church can the person, power, and purpose of Jesus Christ be shared and assimilated. This is what makes our ministry with and to youth unique.

Jesus Christ empowers our kids to live moral lives. Jesus Christ empowers his community—his body—to be a loving, safe, hospitable place. Jesus Christ empowers youth to join the "cloud of witnesses" (Hebrews 12:1) and to proclaim this is God's time, here and now (Luke 4:19). Jesus Christ asks us to be like children and simply believe (Mark 10:15).

There is a particularity to the way Christians must do youth and family ministry. As adults who work with youth, we can shape our programs based upon this primary focus. When I work with congregations, youth, or families that are struggling in their youth ministry, it is nearly always because they lack this focus. Any group of youth and families can go camping, play putt-putt golf, host a bowling party, do service projects, or share in a loving environment. Christians do not have the corner on these activities. What makes our youth activity unique is that we name the NAME. We put the person of Jesus at the center. We let the power of Jesus shape us and our group. We do activities and live our lives in the confidence that they reflect Jesus' purposes.

Youth leaders, pastors, and parents spend enormous amounts of time trying to master the latest techniques such as developing small groups or peer ministries, use the most recent attention-getting gimmick, learn the latest parenting skills, or develop the perfect church-growth strategy. The techniques, the gimmicks, the skill, and the strategies are only as effective as the focus of the leadership.

I close this proverb with my answers to the two opening questions. What is the primary purpose of the church? The primary purpose of the church, as tools of the Holy Spirit, is to help all people discover and grow in faith in Jesus Christ through Christian community for Christ's service. What is the primary purpose of youth and family ministry? The primary purpose of youth and family ministry, as tools of the Holy Spirit, is to help our youth discover and grow in faith in Jesus Christ through Christian community for Christ's service. If this sounds redundant, it is. Youth and family ministry is not some "other thing," different from the larger life of the church. Youth ministry is the essential work of the church at its most basic and important level—EVANGELISM.

Confirmation, church school, youth programs, family ministries, small-group development, peer ministries, contemporary and traditional worship, service projects, camp and retreat outings, mentoring programs, and so forth can be acts of evangelism. I never assume that the youth group or families I am working with are poured-in-concrete believers. Each time we gather I try to tell of Jesus' unconditional love and trust that the Spirit will renew, or kindle for the first time, faith. Belief in Jesus Christ as the person, power, and purpose of our lives is central. It is the Gospel Proverb.

Suggested Strategies

Caring Conversation. Ask these questions: Who has witnessed (shared their faith and the gospel) to you? To whom have you witnessed? How does it feel to tell others about Jesus? What hesitation, if any, do you experience?

Ritual or Tradition. As a part of your autumn Sunday school opening, commission all parents, youth leaders, and adults as evangelists. Use Luke 10:1-12 and 17-20 as the basis for your sermon, hymn selection, and worship. Use this proverb for an education hour conversation. It's also helpful to read Luther's explanation of the Fourth Commandment in the Large Catechism. What is the role of adults in relation to children?

Family/Youth Group Devotion. Read Luke 2:41-52. Jesus shared the word in the temple, although he was young. This astounded the adults. How do you share the word about Jesus? Do your family/friends share the good news? Is it easier to do alone or with others? Are you able to share it better through words or actions?

Servant Event or Retreat. Identify a person with whom you can share your faith. Plan to visit with her or him in the next two weeks, OR, with youth, devise a "Share the Good News" publicity campaign, using posters, meditations in the church newsletter, or other ideas for sharing the good news.

2

Ya Gotta Wanna
The Passion for Youth and Family Ministry Proverb

by Mike Rinehart

> **People who are effective in living and sharing the gospel of Jesus Christ with youth are gifted with a deep care, concern, and interest in children, youth, and families.**

People love to see people of passion. Set yourself on fire and people will come to watch you burn.
Charles Spurgeon

Carolyn was a gifted youth worker. Frustration during her two high school years as president of a struggling youth group gave her a passion for youth ministry and a strong desire to make a youth program work. While studying at a nearby state college she did work in youth ministry with a couple of local congregations. She was quick to build rapport with the youth and parents. When she graduated with a degree in education, they were sorry to see her leave to pursue a full-time position in youth ministry or Christian education.

Grace Church had a struggling youth program much like the church of Carolyn's youth. Once a hub of the area's many youth, the program had diminished until relatively few youth were active. The church had continued to grow with the community, and a part-time director of Christian Education and Youth Ministry was stretched to the limit. Since she did not want to go full-time, the church decided to remove youth ministry from her job description, allowing her to spend all her time on Christian education. Then they began the search process for a full-time director of youth ministry.

Carolyn's roommate had grown up at Grace and relayed the information about the position to Carolyn, also giving Carolyn's name to the church's search committee. Before long they hooked up, and a match was made.

Within a year, the ice began to break. As in college, Carolyn was quick to build relationships with youth and adults alike. Her love for the kids and the gospel, as well as her enthusiasm for the church, were infectious. She went to the schools and had lunch with the youth and made herself available to parents for ideas and support. Her love for service prompted her to plan servant projects locally and trips out of town. Community was built, and word got around.

Two years later, Carolyn fell in love and married a young man in the congregation. Three years after that, her husband got a job transfer out of state, and Carolyn reluctantly resigned. In nearly six years the youth group had more than quadrupled. Youth were active in Bible study, worship, community service, small groups, and even congregational leadership.

Passion in Youth Ministry

The church needed to find someone who could carry on this spectacular ministry. What would it take to find someone as talented as Carolyn? This question is natural, but perhaps not the most helpful. A better question might be, In the future, how can we identify the right person(s) to lead our youth and family ministries?

This question, rarely addressed in youth ministry books and publications, is absolutely crucial to selecting the right candidate(s), especially if hiring for a full-time position. But whether paid or unpaid, full-time or part-time, I usually tell new recruits to youth ministry that all else flows from only two requirements for involvement in youth ministry:

1. You've got to love God.
2. You've got to love kids.

In the end, Carolyn's replacement had more theological training and formal youth ministry training than she. He had taken many courses in running youth programs and had been part of an effective youth group when he was in high school. But Carolyn had something he did not: a fire in her belly. She loved the kids. She loved youth culture with its idiosyncrasies and its energy. She had no preconceived ideas or models for youth ministry, but was willing to try just about anything to make the program work.

Her enthusiasm and energy attracted youth and adults. Her love for the gospel became a model for those with whom she worked. Her leadership could be described as "charismatic leadership" with a strong dose of creativity. When she left, the youth ministry left with her.

For years I believed my job was to create a youth ministry that would remain strong after I left. I now believe this is too idealistic. Would we expect the departure of a good coach to leave a professional football team unchanged? Is the country left unaffected by a new president? Doesn't a new lead singer significantly alter a band's sound?

Charismatic, passionate, highly committed leadership has been at the center of Christian community since its inception. Jesus' leadership is worth books upon books of study. Consider Peter, Paul, Hildegaard de Bingen, John Calvin, Martin Luther, Wesley, Mother Teresa, Martin Luther King Jr. Could any of the movements that they represent have taken hold without their Spirit-led and passionate leadership?

Identifying the Passionate Leader

How do we identify these kinds of leaders? In his book *The Coming Revolution in Youth Ministry*, Mark Senter points out that they are often mavericks. He draws on Tom Peters, author of numerous books on leadership/management. Peters emphatically states that no quantum leap forward has ever come out of the research and development departments of major corporations. He points to Peter Drucker's four crucial leadership traits, listed below. With each trait of what leaders should be or do, I have included comments as to how they relate to youth and family ministry.[1]

1. *Analyzing the opportunities.* Passionate leaders analyze the opportunities for carrying the gospel into youth and family ministry. While so-called leaders ask, "Why?" passionate leaders ask, "Why not?" They are energized by difficult situations and enjoy the challenges inherent in such situations.

2. *Simple and focused.* The ideas of passionate leaders are simple and focused. Like a Mozart symphony, there is a basic, underlying simplicity to their approach that seems obvious in retrospect. They do not attempt to meet every need, but pick one area and excel in it.

3. *Start small and grow.* Passionate leaders start small and grow. They don't model youth programs after the huge church around the corner, but establish an effective niche in the youth and family culture of the congregation and build on it. It begins with a lot of tinkering and adjusting.

4. *Focus on leadership.* Passionate leaders focus on leadership. They are able to attract and hold the loyalty of strong leaders to work with youth and families. As the Spurgeon quote at the beginning of this article intimates, adults and youth are drawn to the charisma and passion of these innovators.

While there is no substitute for competence, it must be said that there is likewise no substitute for passion. Certainly passion combined with compounded incompetence is disastrous, but competence without passion is void of life and spirit. Given the choice of either competence or passion, I'd choose passion in a heartbeat. Think about your relationships. Wouldn't you make the same choice?

Suggested Strategies

Caring Conversation. Ask youth what gives them joy. Ask about their dreams and passions. What recurring themes have surfaced in their lives? Could God be using these passions to guide them to do certain ministries or vocations?

Ritual or Tradition. Read about a different church leader each month for a year, such as Charles Wesley, Martin Luther, Mother Teresa, St. Francis of Assissi, Pope John Paul, and so forth. In what ways has passion and leadership taken place in the history of the church? How do these people communicate their passion?

Family/Youth Group Devotion. Do a family or youth group study of biblical leadership: Moses, Joshua, Samuel, David, Paul. How did these people lead? How was God able to use them? What was the criteria for leadership?

Servant Event or Retreat. Do a "passionate leader" presentation. After studying various Biblical and church leaders, select one or more to "show up" at your church. Dress up as this person and play the role. Develop a speech or presentation each can give.

3

The Family Circle
The Family Proverb

by Anne Marie Nuechterlein

Effective youth leaders recognize that youth are part of larger family systems. In understanding these systems, appropriate and responsive ministries can be developed.

The single most important ingredient in the life of youth is their families.
David Anderson

Youth, like all of us, belong to family systems, and their interactions with one another continually change and evolve. People do not exist in a vacuum, but function interdependently with one another. Their family systems, which include at least three to four generations, maintain their set of rules, roles, expectations, attitudes, myths, forms of communication, power structure, and ways of dealing with conflict.[1]

Youth carry the patterns of their family systems with them into all aspects of their lives. As they get to know new people, they bring their own roles, expectations, and rules with them that have been passed down through the generations. These roles and rules interplay with the roles, expectations, and rules of their various current systems.

For example, fifteen-year-old Amy Briggs's mother, Sue Briggs, called Mark Dupree, the youth director, in a panic because Amy had just told her that she was depressed and thinking about suicide. Sue met with Mark, and in the course of their conversation, Sue told Mark that when she was a teenager, she went through a depressing time. She then told Mark that she was even more scared about Amy's depression because her own father struggled with depression and had attempted suicide when he had been a young man. Mark, who had done some reading about family systems, told Sue that even though depression and thoughts of suicide were a theme in her family over the generations, Sue and Amy could make new choices for themselves about how to deal with their feelings of sadness and depression.

Murray Bowen, a psychiatrist and pioneer in the field of family systems, adds clarity to the discussion of family systems with his concepts of circularity, identified patient, homeostasis, differentiation of self, and emotional triangles.

Circularity

Paul likened the community of faith to the body of Christ, with individual parts making up a whole. In the same way, Bowen's systems theory contends that the whole of the family is greater than the sum of its individual parts. Families are more than individual personalities. Families are a totality in their own right and possess an inner life and existence of their own.

When one member of the body suffers, all members suffer. In the same way, everyone in a family influences one another. All family members play a part in the problems. Family problems are not such that blame can be placed on the one person who is seen as the "cause" of the problem. Instead, all the family members interact in a circular fashion.

For example, in the Huntley family, Chris often takes on the role of the "rebellious child," and Marilyn often takes on the role of the "nagging mother." The more Marilyn nags, the more Chris rebels. Some might say that Chris is a problem child, but family systems theory would say that the issues are much larger than those that appear on the surface. Both Chris and Marilyn receive something out of their behavioral role patterns and, what is more, both will actively work at maintaining their roles.

By ignoring circularity and labeling people, people falsely identify one person as the "victim" or the "problem." When people label others, they categorize them and put them into boxes that sum up their personality or behavioral characteristics in one or two words. If a boy always hears, "You're such a rebellious child," he may take on that behavior. In addition, his parents, family, and teachers may begin viewing him as a rebellious child instead of as someone distinctive, unique, and special.

Identified Patient

When the Israelites celebrated the feast of atonement, they sacrificed a bull to make amends for the sins of the people. They also presented a goat to the priest. The Israelites confessed the sins of their nation and laid them on the goat. They drove the "scapegoat" into the wilderness to suffer death for the community's sins (Leviticus 16:6-22).

Families also identify a "scapegoat," a person who exhibits the most obvious symptoms in the family and takes the blame for the family's problems. Family systems theory refers to this person as the "identified patient." This identified patient is not necessarily the "sick" one, but the one in whom the family's stress or pathology surfaces.[2] When a family member "acts out" the family's dysfunction, that person's pain shows the family's pain. When individuals act out, they cry for help for their family. Thus, the identified patient might be the healthiest one in the family—the one who is trying to keep the family together.

Fourteen-year-old Jason Herzfeld is the identified patient in his family. He acts out the pain in the family system by getting bad grades, ignoring his curfew, causing trouble, and running away from home. His parents think he is the "problem" in the family.

Yet by looking at Jason's actions as expressions of family pain, the Herzfelds could turn their focus to the family and realize that they need help. Through his behavior, Jason says, "I hurt and my family hurts. We suffer enormous pain. Please pay attention and help us." Jason's running away suggests the presence of a serious problem in the family. If a pastor or youth director focuses on Jason's pain rather than that of the family, Jason may experience a superficial healing of his pain and seem to get better. But unless the family pain is addressed, another family member may develop symptoms and become the new identified patient. For instance, his sister might become pregnant or start shoplifting. It is helpful to look at problems with individual family members as symptoms of larger problems in the family system.

Homeostasis

Homeostasis refers to how families seek to maintain their equilibrium. Like a mobile, when one part in a family moves, they all move. Each part moves on its own, but all the parts move, since they all interconnect as a system. Families are similar to mobiles in that when one part moves, all the parts continue to move until they find a new sense of equilibrium or balance.

Both positive and negative changes throw family systems off balance. Families find their homeostasis upset whenever family members exit or enter the family system. Marriages, graduations, births, divorces, and deaths disrupt the family system's balance. These times of joy, excitement, sorrow, and crisis upset the homeostasis and cause family members to experience stress. Changes in the family system's equilibrium often generate anxiety for the family members. The more difficult the transition is, the more noticeable the feelings of panic and anxiety.

A teeter-totter, or seesaw, clarifies the concept of homeostasis. Families maintain their homeostasis when they maintain balance. When somebody experiences change, though, everybody on the family teeter-totter is thrown in the air or on the ground.

When family members lose their balance and homeostasis, they experience pain and discomfort. They also discover an excellent opportunity to examine themselves and make some healthy changes in their family system. Most families, even if they want changes in their family system, find the imbalance distressing and prefer that conditions quickly return to "normal." When families experience a crisis, the initial and comfortable inclination is to figure out how to get things back to "normal." The family, however, might want to use this crisis time to seek outside professional help, not just for the immediate problem, but to make some significant changes that would lead to greater family health.

Jason's running away upset his family's homeostasis. His family, like most families, wanted to fix the problem quickly so that their lives could return to normal. When Jason returned home, his mother called the youth director and asked if she could bring Jason in for counseling to help him with his problems. Trained in family systems theory, the youth director said, "I'll talk with Jason, but I could best help him if the whole family would come in for the first session." She understood that working with Jason might temporarily restore the family to their homeostasis and balance. Yet she knew that unless the family addressed the problems as symptoms of the whole family system, Jason might get better, but another family member would develop a "symptom" or problem to express the pain in their family.

9

Differentiation of Self

While differentiation is an important issue for all of us, it is a particularly strong priority and driving force for teenagers and young adults. When we become differentiated, we live separate and distinct from others, as well as attached and connected to others. We want to help youth and all people be able to really say how they feel, how they think, and how they believe, even if it is different from how others feel, think, or believe.

We want to help youth to be differentiated, that is, to figure out their values and choose their own life course. As youth grow in their identity, they are better able to connect with other people and have a sense of being "me" in their families and communities.

As Christians, God calls us to live out of our God-given identity as differentiated people in relationship with others. When we claim our God-given identity, we recognize who we are as people of God and as individuals and as people in relationship. Our identity includes our values, beliefs, physical characteristics, personality traits, educational background, interests, and profession. Our identity is shaped as we are baptized into Christ. God's words to Jesus apply similarly to us: You are my beloved daughter! You are my beloved son! With you I am well pleased!

Emotional Triangles

Formed by any three persons or issues, an emotional triangle constitutes a basic unit in all family systems. When any two parts of a system become uncomfortable with each other, they "triangle in," or focus upon a third person or issue as a way of stabilizing their relationship with each other. When people are triangulated, they find themselves caught in the middle as the focus of an unresolved issue. When people try to change the relationship of two others (two people, or a person and a belief, problem, or addiction), they triangulate themselves into that relationship.[3] While people want one-to-one relationships with everyone in the family system, two members often pull in, or triangle in, a third person, activity, or situation to decrease the tension and stress in their relationship.

In healthy family systems, a couple has their primary intimate relationship with each other, not with their children. Healthy couples do not share stories, concerns, or secrets with their children that they do not share with each other. To be healthy, family systems need to work consciously at staying out of triangles and work at relating with family members on a personal, one-to-one level.

Conclusion

Who people are in their family systems is a given, but what they do with their family roles, rules, themes, and patterns in their future is up to them. People often discover ways to get healthier when they reflect in a nonjudgmental way about who they are in their families. Through the concepts of circularity, identified patient, homeostasis, differentiation of self, and emotional triangles, people can better understand their family systems.

Understanding one's family system is often a beginning step that can lead to change. Gaining new insights about ourselves and our families enables us to make new decisions about who we are, who we want to be, and how we want to live our lives. Once we understand our family patterns, roles, and rules, we can make intentional choices about which patterns, roles, and rules enhance our lives, and which patterns, roles, and rules detract from our lives.[4]

Suggested Strategies

Caring Conversation. Talk about your family system. How would you complete these sentences?

1. The things I like most about our family are…

2. I wish our family would change in these ways…

3. My ideal family would…

Ritual or Tradition. What rituals and traditions are important to you in your family? Think in terms of holidays, birthdays, weekend activities, evening routines, and mealtimes. What rituals and traditions would you like to develop in your family?

Family/Youth Group Devotion. In what ways can family devotions be helpful as you grow together as a family? What kind of devotional format might be most enjoyable and enriching for your family? Identify a family in the Bible that yours is most like. For example, explore Mary and Joseph's relationship and family (Matthew 1:18-25). Check out a really dysfunctional family, the family of David (2 Samuel 11:1—12:23; 13:1-39).

Servant Event or Retreat. Plan a weekly family retreat. Mark a time each week when the whole family turns off the television, computer, and phone and reads, plays a game, watches and discusses a movie, is active outdoors, and/or talks together. Plan to take three hours. Call it a D.E.A.R. event (Drop Everything and Retreat). Make sure to include a family devotion. For example, look up the word *retreat* in a Bible concordance and see how it is used.

4

I Really Love You, Friend!
The Relationship Proverb

by Mike Rinehart

Effective youth and family ministry takes place in a dynamic, relational partnership between youth, adults, families, staff, volunteers, role models, and mentors who represent multiple generations.

It takes an entire village to raise a single child.
African Proverb

More often than not, children are learning major value systems in life from the horizontal peer-culture. The vertical structure is not there in adequate increment of time or intensity to do the job.
Gordon MacDonald

Megan Wilson doesn't spend much time with adults. Today the alarm goes off at 6:15 in the morning, setting in motion a series of events that explode upon her day at a furious pace. During her morning ritual, she sees her mother (a single parent) for about 15 minutes while hurriedly wolfing down a bowl of cereal. She makes it to the bus stop by 7:30 A.M.

At school she listens to the teachers lecture, but has little one-on-one interaction with them. After school she stays for pom-poms, which is led entirely by youth. Her boyfriend picks her up and takes her home. Mom will get home from work around 6:00 P.M. By then she is out with friends.

When she gets home at 8:45 P.M., Mom is winding down and ready for bed. After a brief conversation with her mom (frequently interrupted by her younger sister), she sits down in front of the television and pulls out the books and begins work on some homework that is due tomorrow. By 11:30 P.M. she is in bed. She has spent 45 minutes with her mother (this is about the national average). What's interesting is that two generations ago, her grandfather would have spent most of the day with his father (working on the farm). Clearly, those days are gone.

Consider this: 45% of the world is under 19 years of age. That's a huge chunk of the population. These are the adults of tomorrow. Who is mentoring them? Who is teaching them civic responsibility, compassion, self-esteem, or patience? Who is the hero or the mentor for them to emulate? Could it be the rock star or the television star? Who is devoting hours of time and care in the lives of our children?

Hello, America!

Mark DeVries has provided us with a wake-up call in the form of his book, *Family-Based Youth Ministry*. His premise is that we've put far too much weight on the nuclear family. We need to help and support the nuclear family with the extended Christian family of the church. This is what our new youth ministries need to be about. Youth and family ministry must grow out of a dynamic interaction between youth, young adults, and older adults. And he has some pretty good research to back it up.

DeVries quotes Cornell University's Uri Bronfenbrenner, citing nine societal changes that have separated youth from adults:

- fathers' vocational choices that remove them from the home for lengthy periods of time
- an increase in the number of working mothers
- a critical escalation in the divorce rate
- a rapid increase in single-parent families
- a steady decline in the extended family
- the evolution of the physical environment of the home (family rooms, play-rooms, and master bedrooms)
- the replacement of adults by the peer group
- the isolation of children from the work world
- the insulation of schools from the rest of society[1]

Or consider these eye-opening sound bytes: American parents spend less time with their children than parents in any other country of the world. One in four young people indicate that they have never had a meaningful conversation with their father. Three in four teens actually want their parents to spend more time with them. Perhaps what this means for youth ministry is a greater commitment to help parents and other adult caregivers to connect on a personal level with the daily life and faith development of youth.

A few years ago my church generously offered me a three-month sabbatical. I chose to do some research in youth culture that involved several focus groups in various parts of the country. One of my good friends—a dedicated youth pastor—and I developed a series of questions about what it is like to be a high school–age youth in today's world. We looked to current research to get our primary information and then did the focus groups to back up the information and put a "face" on the information.

In group after group I had the same experience. For two to three hours the youth enthusiastically and tirelessly answered my questions. Frankly, I was shocked. I had spent hours developing classes and youth meetings that could keep their over-schooled minds attentive, and I rarely succeeded dramatically. But here I was commanding the attention of six to ten youth without saying hardly anything.

Finally, I asked one of the youth why he participated in the group with such rapt attention. His response was simple: "I don't think any adult has ever sat and listened to me nonjudgmentally for two hours before." He was as shocked with me as I was with him. We simply do not have enough intergenerational interaction in our culture. We are too segmented.

Churches are notorious for this. Many families report that they don't see one another for two hours after they walk in the door of the church. We suck individuals into age-specific classes and activities, so that there is very little "family time" left in parish life. Instead of empowering the family to be a center for faith and spirituality, we often add to the hectic pace and separation that families experience on a daily basis.

Turning the Tide

How can we turn the tide on this negative downward spiral? We need to adopt an approach to youth ministry that focuses on relationships instead of programs. Programs come and go, but everyone knows (especially the youth) that it's relationships that make it or break it for any ministry. This new approach would move away from making well-attended youth events the goal, to establishing long-lasting, trusting relationships between youth, parents, younger adults, and older adults. (This is not really a new model, but the very oldest.)

Youth ministry would not be a ministry to the youth. Rather, it would be a ministry carried on between adults and youth, recognizing the ministry that youth bring to adults as well as the ministry adults bring to youth. Lutheran Youth Encounter, based in Minneapolis, Minnesota, has a mission statement that reflects this important focus. Their purpose is "to strengthen the church through the faith of its youth."

This approach recognizes not only the desperate need of our youth for adult mentoring, but also the reality that, biblically, their faith is considered a role model for adults. Jesus says that unless we have the faith of a child, we will never see the kingdom of God. Jesus understands that faith is relational, and perhaps young people have a better sense of that than adults!

Fleshing It Out

This is the part where we get down to specifics. What would this look like in a real setting? I'm just going to brainstorm aloud. Some of these things have been tried with great success and others are "hot off the press."
- Coordinate the topics/Bible studies for Sunday school so that youth, children, and adults are all on the same topic, and so will spark family discussions at home
- Multigenerational Sunday school
- Family choir
- Small groups for single-parent families, only-child families, and so forth
- Professionally led and peer-led support groups for families in crisis
- Fewer activities; more family outings
- Providing worship in the musical idiom of the people
- Older adult mentors for all young people
- More materials that help parents teach the Bible and tenets of the faith at home
- More family devotional material: teach the Four Keys (see preface)
- Start an "Adopt a Grandparent" program at your church for families who are separated from their grandparents by many miles
- Go back to the good old parent or guardian/child banquets

- Line or square dancing for the older adults groups and the elementary youth group
- Youth on every committee at the church
- Have classes in which you teach the parents, but test kids

I hope these ideas get the creative juices flowing. More important than what programs you start will be how you think your way through the process. Always begin with this crucial question: Are we focusing on relationships and community?

Suggested Strategies

Caring Conversation. Just for the fun of it, come up with a questionnaire for your youth. Invite parents to add their questions. Ask everything you want (and don't want) to know about teen life (top 10 challenges, people they trust/don't trust, and so forth). Tell them they can write the answers or share them with you verbally. (Nine out of ten will choose the latter.) Not only will this foster good conversation, but it will also communicate that you really care and are interested in their lives. Share what you've learned with parents. Make sure you protect confidentiality.

Ritual or Tradition. Get kids together with their grandparents or surrogate grandparents and talk about special relationships they have. What makes them special? Do this on All Saints Sunday and explain that this is the Sunday in the church year when we remember those who shared the faith through their relationships and now have joined the saints eternal.

Family/Youth Group Devotion. Read John 1:35-49. How did Andrew come to be a disciple? Simon? Philip? Nathanael? Note how all followed Jesus because they received an invitation to "come and see" from someone they already knew. They had a prior relationship with their discipleship recruiter. Discuss who invited or invites you to come and see. Whom have you invited?

Servant Event or Retreat. Plan a church clean-up day or community servant project with only youth and senior citizens. Assign work teams that keep youth and seniors working side by side.

5

The Youngest in Our Midst
The Early Childhood Proverb

by Susan K. Sherwood

> **The season of early childhood is a time when a myriad of experiences lay the foundation for the physical, emotional, cognitive, and social growth necessary for faith development.**

To every thing there is a season, and a time to every purpose under the heaven.
Ecclesiastes 3:1 KJV

Andrea Michelle, born October 7, at 5:50 A.M., weighed six pounds and seven ounces. The miracle of birth ushered a child into the season of early childhood. That event graced the world with another human being full of tremendous potential, and blessed me with the joy of motherhood. At this retelling, nearly two decades later, I must confess I felt compelled to make Andrea a child of God without realizing the urgency of that mission.

I am thankful my own nurturing, caring, faith-filled mother provided me with an exemplary role model, for she instinctively revered the potential of each of God's children, even when they were the youngest in our midst. She considered her children seedlings to be nurtured and tended each day. Her legacy to me preceded my study of the burgeoning recent research in the study of the human brain and in the field of child development. In only the last decade, we have learned that at birth an infant's brain has 100 billion building blocks, called neurons, and 50 trillion synapses, which form pathways between neurons to allow all the areas of the brain to communicate and function together. The neurons and the synapses that connect them make up the "wiring" of the brain. During the first year of life, the number of synapses will explode to 1,000 trillion and then by approximately age 10 decline to only 500 trillion, roughly the same number as the average adult.[1] If the brain's capacity is not used, it is lost. "To every thing there is a season, and a time to every purpose under the heaven" (Ecclesiastes 3:1 KJV); thus, this season of early childhood must not pass without our preparing the soil and planting the seeds necessary for faith development.

To set the stage for extending this agrarian metaphor, we must recognize the vitality of an infant at birth. The wiring between neurons is already complete for vital functions like heartbeat and breathing and for some of our children's inherited attributes, like temperament and mannerisms. Other connections, like those that constitute sight and sound, are more frail. For these neural pathways to become strong, the brain depends on sensorial and stimulating experiences, such as the sight of a smile or the sound of a hymn. Simple acts that were instinctive exchanges from one generation to the next in our family were building blocks for brain development.

As we prepare the soil, we are setting the groundwork for the growth cycle and brain development. It is those early experiences that have a dramatic impact on the child's growth and development processes. The role of caring adults is critical to the child's development through these experiences! On a daily basis, caring adults meet the basic needs and provide a wide range of developmentally appropriate experiences essential for infants and young children. For example, getting one's needs met is the early task of an infant. The child cries and is constantly aware whether the needs for food and comfort are being ignored or responded to in a loving manner. If the responses from the adult are consistent and predictable, the seeds are sown for the child to feel secure, and trust will develop. If, however, the cries are ignored or met with harsh words or rough handling, the child will have difficulty developing trust. Children who have not developed a sense of trust are unable to attach and focus on trying to get their needs met in healthy ways. They will often develop many fears that are not rational. This will limit their opportunities for exploring and experiencing the wonders of the surrounding world.

Experiencing the warmth and responsiveness of the caregiver in the early months of life forms the roots of emotional development. Very young children learn to know touch and warmth: a kiss on the forehead, a tender stroke of the cheek. If children are deprived of warmth, including touch, infants will not develop trust and not be able to use warmth and touch in their human communication; however, children who experience consistent and loving patterns of attention develop trust, enabling them to attach to an individual.

The caring adult nurtures and tends growth through mediating a myriad of experiences. This vital mediation is a part of continued cognitive development that allows the child to blossom. Mediation occurs when adults interact with children about objects, concepts, and experiences. Being intentional as the child plays with a ball, an adult might say: "I see you are playing with the red ball. That's the ball that Grandma gave you for your birthday. Tomorrow we'll take the ball to the park and play catch." Through this mediated experience focusing on the concept of time, the adult has given that specific ball a past, the one Grandma gave you for your birthday; and a future, the one we'll take to the park and play catch with tomorrow. As the child begins to understand the past in order to construct the present, the construction of the future is also possible. In addition to time, concepts such as position, spatial relationships, representation, sequences, and consequences are essential for healthy intellectual development. These critical cognitive processes are prerequisites to the development of beliefs and spiritual understanding.

By the time a child reaches the age of three, the basic patterns for spiritual development are ingrained. The early years are a time of gathering children in to participate, observe, and imitate. Activities such as eating a meal with the family, getting ready for bed, and going to church provide traditions, routines, and worship experiences that are associated with religious beliefs and spiritual life; clearly, the practices associated with these activities must be internalized during the early years. These social experiences are the underpinnings for all future spiritual development. As children watch others, they copy their behaviors. Going to church and seeing others singing and praying are powerful images. When significant people in their lives share their faith and spiritual life in actions and words, children witness a blueprint for their faith development. As they observe and imitate behaviors, it is essential that caring adults provide age-appropriate explanations of symbols and activities, as well as affirmation of the child's actions. Through this dialogue, children develop a sense of self-worth and competence.

As stewards of the earth and all that is within, we as a congregation have an incredible responsibility for God's children. We need to take an active role preparing the soil, planting the seeds, nurturing, and tending the growth of and gathering in each child in our midst. By supporting and encouraging those families who understand the importance of development, and by teaching and modeling for those who have not had the legacy of love, we can make a difference. We must focus energies and resources to make all children feel welcome. As parents and as members of a church family, we must start at birth and continue to nurture development throughout childhood. Furthermore, we must be intentional about providing those experiences in the church fellowship and the neighborhood that will lay the foundation for physical, emotional, cognitive, and social growth necessary for faith development. Proverbs 22:6 (KJV) says, "Train up a child in the way he should go: and when he is old, he will not depart from it"—and that works best when you start at birth.

Suggested Strategies

Caring Conversation. How welcome are children in your church? Brainstorm a list of responses and classify them as "Children Are Welcomed" or "Children Are Not Welcomed." How do you welcome newborns and their families into our congregation? How might you expand the ways you welcome children? What additional opportunities might you include for children to participate in worship? One church has added knee-high door handles to all the church doors. This says, "Children are welcome!" What other ways can you be infant/child friendly?

Ritual or Tradition. Send baptismal anniversary cards to each child. Make sure you include a prayer that the parent(s) can pray with their child at home. This can serve as a reminder to each child of the day she or he became a child of God. Publish these special dates in the church bulletin and remember them during worship in prayer.

Family/Youth Group Devotion. Use Matthew 18:3-5 as the basis for devotions. Lead a discussion about what it means to change and become like a little child. Share your earliest childhood memories. How did you experience parents, peers, and church? What were your images of God?

Servant Event or Retreat. Encourage youth and adults to "adopt" an infant or young child. Relationships can be developed and nurtured during regularly scheduled church worship and events; they have the potential to extend outside the church setting. These bonds can be enriching for infants and young children and rewarding for youth and adults.

6

I Have a Dream!
The Vision Proverb

by Paul Hill

> An effective youth and family ministry has a guiding vision. This vision is discerned through prayer and the cooperative efforts of church leaders, adults, parents, and youth. The vision is broadly owned.

I will pour out my Spirit upon all flesh, and your sons and daughters shall prophesy, and your young men shall see visions, and your old men shall dream dreams.
Acts 2:17

All youth leaders should watch the movie *The Blues Brothers* with their youth and families. Everything we need to know about the Vision Proverb is there. Jake and Elwood are the Blues Brothers on a "mission for God." The sunglasses, the white shirts, the identical suits, and the '50s dress hats make up the costumes of our two mission-driven rock 'n' rollers. They are called—compelled—to raise money to save an orphanage. To accomplish their mission they need to "put the band together again." In the process they endure police harassment, multiple car chases, murder attempts by a whacky former girlfriend, and SWAT team attacks. Finally, not even a cold, insensitive bureaucracy can deter them, and their mission is fulfilled. Jake and Elwood have a vision with a specific mission. Their mission was to save the orphanage; their vision was to help kids have a safe, loving, caring place to live. They complete their immediate mission; the vision lives on. (Thus the justification for sequels in the movie business.)

To have a vision is to have power. To have a vision is to be powerful. To have a vision that is of God is to lead with power. Martin Luther, Mother Teresa, and Dr. Martin Luther King Jr. each had a vision. For Luther it was of a church that does not sell Jesus, but shares Jesus. For Mother Teresa it was a vision of God who calls God's people to care for the outcasts. For Dr. King it was a dream of a common humanity rooted in mutual respect. Their visions have moved nations, institutions, and millions of people. Importantly, none of these people held political office, commanded armies, or possessed great wealth. Yet their accomplishments have reshaped the world. Vision is that powerful and that important.

Vision is not the same as optimism. In youth ministry this distinction is critical. Ministry with youth that repeatedly emphasizes being "up," "high," or "whoopin' and screamin'" teaches our kids that Christians are basically adrenaline addicts. There is a vital place for this kind of ministry. It's fun, it takes us to the mountain top, it lifts our spirits. We need times like that. However, it is an incomplete youth and family ministry experience.

Optimism is emotion. Vision is commitment. Optimism is immediate. Vision takes the long view. Most kids are naturally optimistic simply because of youthful energy. Life has a way of wearing those youthful batteries down. Therefore, a special gift we can give our youth and our youth ministries is a vision that sustains us when the emotion is gone, the fatigue has set in, the problems are piling up, and the money has run out. Vision provides purpose, a reason for being, a reason for doing, a reason for sacrificing, a reason for thinking beyond the self. Vision is like the little engine that could. It just keeps plugging along, sometimes in unspectacular ways, getting the job done in spite of changes in personnel, bad weather, poor track conditions, and less-than-appreciative participants. Vision sustains us long after the adrenaline has left our bloodstream.

Jesus has a vision. It is outlined clearly in Luke 4:18-19. Jesus comes to the synagogue, opens the Hebrew scripture, and reads from Isaiah:

> The Spirit of the Lord is upon me,
> because he has anointed me to bring good news to the poor.
> He has sent me to proclaim release to the captives
>   and recovery of sight to the blind,
>   to let the oppressed go free,
> to proclaim the year of the
>   Lord's favor.

The rest of the story of Luke and Acts (written by the same author) is a running illustration of how Jesus makes this vision come alive. The prodigal son is welcomed home; the sick and infirm are healed; the hungry are fed; the 70 are sent; Jesus is crucified, raised, and reveals himself on the road to Emmaus; the Holy Spirit comes at Pentecost; the ministry goes out to Jews and Greeks. All of this activity is driven by the vision Jesus claims for himself in the synagogue on that earth-changing day. Visions are big.

In 1929 Christian educator George Albert Coe said, "Shall the primary purpose of Christian education [ministry to youth] be to hand on a religion, or to create a new world?" This is the question of vision. How we answer this question will determine every aspect of our ministry. In seeing our youth and family ministry as part of "creating a new world," we grasp a larger vision. Jesus Christ's death and resurrection on the cross is a new beginning for us and for the cosmos.

Those who share this vision move beyond immediate institutional concerns to a larger reality. This larger reality shapes our ministry much differently. We recognize that Jesus Christ's person, power, and purpose can work across denominational lines. Most of this generation does not understand denominational differences anyway and couldn't care less. Ecumenical cooperation is a must. With this vision our youth are seen not as the future, but as people in ministry now, with gifts to give and a calling to fulfill. Peer ministry is a good example of how this vision could shape a program. We ask, "How can we equip our youth to serve one another?" I believe this is exactly what God does in the incarnation as Jesus—Immanuel, God with us.

The vision of creating a new world leads us to look for ways that our youth can live and share the faith in school and school-related activities, rather than continuously offering competing programs for youth with limited time and full schedules. The prayer pole idea is one such example. Christian youth gather outside of their schools around the flag pole and pray together each day. It's legal, relevant, and a powerful witness.

Creating a new world means that families do not exist to support the church; rather, the church exists to support the families. The best youth programs are those that help parents be evangelists to their own children. Christian parenting classes, family devotional materials, and support groups for parents and youth at risk are examples of how this larger vision can take shape (see David Anderson's preface).

A congregation in southern Wisconsin located near a poor elementary school developed a morning breakfast program for the children who attended that school. Teachers had reported that none of the children learned much until after lunch, because few of them came to school having had breakfast. The move to reach out to these children in this way was extremely controversial to the membership because of the racist attitudes towards the children. Nevertheless, a breakfast program was begun and the teachers quickly reported how much better the children were doing in school. Soon an after-school program took shape, and within a couple of years a summer program also developed. The congregation survived the battle and now celebrates this new and larger youth ministry. There is a sense of ownership across the board. More important, the neighborhood children are benefiting. Will they gain more members from this move? Some have joined, but not many as of yet. Does the program pay for itself? No. The congregation must subsidize it. Is Jesus' vision taking shape? Most assuredly.

The Vision Proverb calls us to think big—as big as God thinks. Those who grasp the vision have a difficult challenge. They must live in two worlds. The world they can see in their mind's eye and the world that would shrink their vision. Although this is not a typical "how to" book, let me share one helpful strategy for success in growing a vision. The key to success in developing and implementing a vision for youth and family ministry requires bringing into the conversation a broad spectrum of people from the congregation and community. Second, before the conversation on vision develops, take time to do activities that build trust between the participants. The detractors, the youth, the parents, the pastors, the staff, and the community leaders need to become friends. Only in this context can a larger vision take shape. Third, study scripture together. What is God's vision for God's people? Finally, try not to put yourself into the position of selling a vision to a skeptical audience that isn't buying. Rather, invite people to become partners—mutual visionaries—and encourage their input. This takes time. It's not unusual for this process to take from one to three years. However, once everyone owns the vision, things move quickly and energy and resources become available because everyone is behind it. Everyone is helping to create a new world.

Suggested Strategies

Caring Conversation. Can you identify a person for whom you have great respect? What is his or her vision for living? If you don't know, ask him or her to find out. How did he or she come to have this vision of life?

Family/Youth Group Devotion. Invite each family/youth group member to identify a Bible passage that says something that is important about his or her vision in life. Pull all these thoughts together and write a vision statement that includes all. How does this statement keep you on a mission for God?

Ritual or Tradition. Revisit and review your youth group/family vision statement every three months. How has this vision been lived out in specific instances and situations? How can you update it for the future?

Servant Event or Retreat. What three service projects (such as working in a food pantry, helping elderly people, recycling materials, making gift baskets for college students) can your youth/family group do in the next six months that illustrates your living out God's vision for you?

7
Light in Our Darkness
The New Hope Proverb

by Ralph Quere

Youth and families need a sense of hope, purpose, and identity. Discovery of hope, purpose, and identity grounded in the gospel is the primary spiritual goal of youth and family ministry.

For I am certain that nothing…in all creation…will ever be able to separate us from the love of God which is ours through Christ Jesus our Lord.
Romans 8:38-39 TEV

We walked out of the hospital in the dark of night—one of the darkest nights of my life. I said to my wife, "The devil won again!" I was angry at God! I felt like shaking my fist at the heavens.

We had been awakened in the middle of the night to be told that—about 12 hours after surgery—our infant son had taken a turn for the worse. As we drove to the hospital, I knew for the first time what it meant that shepherds "quaked" with fear. By the time we arrived, Davey was dead.

We already knew that, since our first child also had died from a similar birth defect, it would be unwise to give birth to any more children. We were at a dark dead end without much hope. We seemed to be in the situation Plato described: life hemmed in by past memories and future expectations that were negative and fearful.[1] But in the Old Testament, trust linked to hope creates positive expectations. Expecting God to step into our deadly situation means yearning and desiring, yet being willing to wait—ready for a fight against evil or a flight to God, who is our safe space.[2]

In the face of a defeat like death, the New Testament counsels not against grief, but against grieving like those "who have no hope" (1 Thessalonians 4:13). Paul continues in 1 Thessalonians 5:4-10 to teach that where there is no hope of eternal life we can be overwhelmed by the threat of death. This threat of death—by drugs or drive-by shootings, suicide or accident, alcohol or AIDS, epidemic or disaster—allows us to understand the psalmist's question, "Why are you cast down, O my soul?" (Psalm 42:5), but how do we grab the psalmist's answer, "Hope in God" (Psalm 42:11)? We remain without hope and without God in this world if we are without Jesus Christ. For his death brings us into God's presence and makes our peace with God (Ephesians 2:12-19).

Youth and families need this hope to face with courage the evil that confronts them—inside and outside themselves in the devil, the world, and the sinful self. To the Old Testament understanding of hope as heartfelt desire and patient waiting, the New Testament adds trust and expectation[3] in Jesus as God's fulfillment of the ancient promise of God's rescue of the whole creation. In that hope made real in Jesus we dare to trust. Because God kept that promise, we dare to expect God will keep all the rest.

Such hope brings youth not only confidence, but also purpose—a sense of calling. There is even hope connected with this call (Ephesians 4:4). Sharing the message of Christ with the hopeless also makes the message more real to the messenger. When the Spirit switches on the light, we can see the hope that we are inheriting from the Father of glory (Ephesians 1:17-18).

About a year after we adopted our daughter, Cyndie, she was admitted to the hospital where Davey had died. There Cyndie was diagnosed with rheumatoid arthritis. The symptoms disappeared for three years and then reappeared, but the prognosis was that she would undoubtedly outgrow it. It has never reoccurred. That memory of God's healing power fuels our hope now. For after her second child was born, Cyndie developed breast cancer that was successfully treated with a mastectomy and chemotherapy. The cancer reappeared two and one-half years later—this time treated by a difficult bone-marrow transplant. Again God's healing power worked through medical procedure. We continue to trust and pray; we hope and we wait for final adoption and full redemption, which have not yet arrived (Romans 8:19-25). Because we are still surrounded by suffering, we need the patient endurance that produces strong character, which in turn gives us hope (Romans 5:1-5; 12:2).

We trust not only God's promise, presence, and power: we trust Christ himself as "our hope" (1 Timothy 1:1; see also Colossians 1:27 and Matthew 12:21). By faith in Jesus as our friend, our brother, and our hero, hope becomes real in our life and experience. At critical periods, youth often judge the church boring! Our worship needs new expressions of the joy of salvation that communicate better with youth. We need to let the powerful words of grace be "audible sacraments" (Pelikan), as well as "visible words" (Augustine). Contemporary music and drama are vehicles to carry watery, edible, drinkable gospel promises to youth. When these gifts are delivered, the Spirit uses them as tools to create faith. For faith comes from the word youth hear concerning Christ—indeed the word coming from Christ himself (Romans 10:8-17). And faith makes hope real and sure. Faith alone gives form and shape to our hopes (Hebrews 11:1). In Romans 15:5-6, 13, Paul says that the steadfastness and encouragement of the scriptures bring hope, for the God of steadfastness and encouragement grants us unity of purpose, and that our "God of hope" gives "joy and peace in believing" so that we may abound in hope by the power of the Holy Spirit. Such hope is our goal and our destiny.

Suggested Strategies

Caring Conversation. Have you ever known anyone without hope? Have you ever felt that way? When someone dies too young—by violence, accident, or disease—how can expressing grief open us to experiencing hope? Who can you talk to when you feel hopeless? What drives you to feel hopeless or hopeful? What things give you hope?

Ritual or Tradition. Identify the various ways hope is shared every day through our greetings (such as Shalom, God's peace, Good-bye, God be with ye, Keep the faith, Peace, and so forth). Select one of these hope-bearing greetings or make up one and share it with all.

Family/Youth Group Devotion. The New Hope Proverb is rooted in the Reformation's Scripture principle. Discuss how Psalm 119 is a gold mine of hope for youth (see especially verses 43, 49, 74, 81, 114, and 116). Study the Ephesians passages referred to in the article, especially 1:15-23; 2:11-22; and 4:1-7. How is hope related to Jesus? How do the Romans texts (5:1-11; 8:18-28; 12:9-21; and 15:1-31) help us deal with sufferings and evil in the world and still stay hopeful?

Servant Event or Retreat. Visit with an elderly person. Ask him or her what gives him or her hope. When in his or her life did he or she feel hopeless? How does God help him or her be hopeful?

8

God Was a Concept Until We Went over the Falls Together
The Experiencing God Proverb

by Paul Hill

> **Effective youth and family ministry incorporates a holistic approach to learning and faith sharing. Opportunities to learn and grow in faith are offered in interactive, active, hands-on, relational, and experiential ways.**

Tell me and I will forget; show me and I may remember; involve me and I will understand.
Anonymous

As a young teen of 15 I went on a 25-day canoe trip into the Boundary Waters Canoe Area of northern Minnesota and southern Canada. (I still can't believe my mother let me go!) I had much to learn, including the infamous canoeing J stroke. Anyone who wants to stern (steer) a canoe must learn the difficult, but essential, J stroke.

My best friend from high school, Greg, also was on this trip. One day waterfalls and rapids lay ahead of us, requiring that we portage our canoes and equipment around that dangerous water. To reach the portage trail, we first had to paddle across the current above the falls to get to the trailhead. Having navigated this tricky maneuver, I was unloading our canoe when I suddenly heard our guide screaming at Greg's canoe, "J stroke! J stroke on the left, hard!" I turned to see poor Greg trying to master this confounded paddle stroke even as the current was taking him and his terrified bowman to the brink. Greg mastered the J stroke in the span of about five seconds. They came close to the brink, but they made it to the portage. The J stroke was no longer an intellectual exercise for elite canoeists. It was a skill necessary for survival.

It is essential that we help our youth and families develop the skill to look for God in all life experiences and preferably not only when they are on the brink. In discerning God in their experiences, faith is no longer a cold, intellectual doctrine; it is the ability to see hope in life. Sterile, academic confirmation programs would do well to follow this proverb. Rather than provide answers for questions the youth are not asking, we should search together for meaning to questions they are asking.

Effective youth ministers intentionally create settings and situations where God is experienced. Bible stories, theological inquiries, and faith questions take on personal meaning for youth through hands-on experience and interactive conversation. Brother Thomas provides an illustration for us:

Brother Thomas was driving our youth group through the hills of northern Mexico. A vehement, constantly talking (preaching), fundamentalistic Christian, Brother Thomas was in his element. We were traveling (captured) with him in a van on our way to visiting a small village to lead a worship service. As we rounded a bend in the road, a woman crossed in front of us, forcing the van to slow down.

"See that woman?" asked Brother Thomas.
"Uh huh," groaned the group.
"She was a Catholic nun…before she was saved," Brother Thomas triumphantly announced.

Eyes met eyes, questions in all of them, and a long, long silence followed. My wife and I cringed from this theologically arrogant statement. Not much else happened until that evening.

Our group met for the end-of-the-day debriefing time. It didn't take long before Brother Thomas's comment was mentioned.
Youth #1: I didn't know Catholics were not saved.
Youth #2: Who says they aren't saved?
Youth #1: But Brother Thomas said that nun on the road wasn't saved.
Youth #3: She's saved; she just had to be born again.
Youth #1: Catholics aren't born again?
Youth #2: They are born again, but not the way Brother Thomas thinks about it.
Youth #4: So, are we saved?
(As the pastor who confirmed this youth, I was in deep despair to hear this question.)
Youth #2: I think everyone is saved.
(As the pastor who confirmed this youth, I was in deep despair to hear this answer.)
Youth #5: I think Brother Thomas is an idiot. Where are the chips?
(As the pastor who confirmed this youth, I was in deep despair.)

No amount of cognitive work in confirmation or the classroom can replace the live, "in-your-face" conversation that experience generates. Brother Thomas did our group a tremendous favor. His remark triggered a conversation that endured throughout our trip. Our youth probed the question of salvation for hours. Luther's Small Catechism was even brought into the discussion. Theological discussion in the context of life experience is the primary place where we discover God.

In the mid-'80s, Barneveld, Wisconsin, was blown off the map by a tornado. People were killed. The town was demolished. Pastor Jeff, living in a nearby town, saw the tragedy and the ministry that this situation presented. He rounded up his youth group and they headed to Barneveld for a week of work. Their primary task was to pick up items blown into the corn fields so that they would not jam the combines in the fall.

The youth asked, "Where is God in all of this?" "Did God do this intentionally?" "Why do these things happen?" "Doesn't God care?" "Why do bad things happen?" "Why do bad things happen to me?"

Pastor Jeff reports that the week in Barneveld was one of the best youth group weeks he has ever experienced. Senior high youth have two major needs: the need to be needed and the need for identity. Their servant time in Barneveld addressed both needs. The youth were engaged, intense, and experiencing the mystery of God.

There is a strong tendency and history among Christians to try to shelter their youth from the realities of God's world. Some Christian youth ministry has the look and feel of trying to create a protective enclave from sinful, secular surroundings. This is not ministry, but a form of denial, a practice in which our culture has a great deal of expertise. It is neither possible nor a good idea to do this.

We cannot protect our youth from the potholes on life's road; we can help them develop a good set of Christian shock absorbers. We don't want to create naive Christians; we want to create Christians who see the nativity in the midst of the world's ugliness, challenges, and questions. We can "get real" or we can "get irrelevant."

This is not to say that we throw our youth to the world and ask what they have learned about God. Issues of safety, morality, law, and common sense must be observed. The Experiencing God Proverb is about a mutual pilgrimage. The key to this book is adults walking with youth, embracing and helping them think through their experiences. These adults are pilgrimage partners. People on a pilgrimage don't have all the answers, but they know how to look and think about their journey. All Christians are on such a pilgrimage. Pilgrimage partners bring youth along with them. Most importantly, pilgrimage partners ask this question: Where have you seen God today? This question frames the youth's experiences in a caring, safe, inquisitive, and interactive adult relationship. Youth are helped to see God as real and to experience God because we encourage them to look for and identify God in their daily lives.

Tony was a tough kid. By the age of eight, he had seen a friend shot to death on the streets of Chicago. By 17, he was cynical, guarded, doing poorly in an alternative high school, using a lot of drugs, and isolated. Tony was part of a group of at-risk youth that I lead through some adventure-based, experiential, team-building exercises. Tony was smart, with strong leadership skills. One day I asked him, "Tony, has anyone ever told you that you are bright and lead well?"

"No," was his grunted response.

"Well, you are!"

Later the same day Tony's teacher called me and asked what I said to him. I told him and wondered if there was a problem. "No, it's just that he has been floating around the high school all day, saying, 'Paul says I'm a smart leader.'"

Tony had received affirmation. From such an experience I did hope to introduce Tony to the affirmation of Jesus Christ.

The following week Tony acted out so badly in our class that we had to stop the activities for the day. What happened? Who knows. However, I *know* that God works in our world and there will be a time to connect the experiences for Tony.

The Bible contains many stories of people who are smart and have leadership skills, and who insist on acting out—resisting and refusing to see God in their reality. The Bible contains also the stories of parents, mentors, peers, youth, or groups—theological teachers of life's experiences—showing us God not as an abstract concept, but as a living reality in the midst of those experiences.

Suggested Strategies

Caring Conversation. Invite a group of older Christians to sit in with your youth group or family. Ask them to come prepared with a story or anecdote that tells when and how they experienced God. Break the stories into two parts. The first part retells the experience including the who, what, when, where, and how parts. Ask the group or family members to retell the story in their small groups to make sure they have all the details. Then ask them to reflect upon the why question. Why did this experience happen? Why would God allow or do this? Why would this be a story about experiencing God? Bring the group back together again and have the group share their responses to the why questions. Ask the original storyteller to share her or his answer to the questions. How do the various answers compare? Has or is anyone in the group had or having a similar experience?

Ritual or Tradition. Establish "experiencing God" holidays. We experience God every day, yet some experiences seem more profound and significant. Ask each member of the family to recall a time when she or he had a profound experience of God. Try to recall the details of this event. Mark your family calendar with the anniversary dates of these events. On those special days have a holiday celebration. Prayers can be written that mark the event and special songs sung or listened to. Create an experiencing God instant replay event through story, pictures, video, drawings and art, poetry, and so forth. Write a liturgy or psalm that the family can read responsively in honor of this special experiencing of God. These holidays can be updated, changed, and remembered anew, because God never stops trying to touch us.

Family/Youth Group Devotion. Try a guided imagery or meditation. Guided imagery directs our thoughts to an experience of God. It can be done anywhere as long as there are no interruptions. For example, have a person pick his or her favorite New Testament Bible story. Ask everyone to get into a comfortable sitting position, close their eyes, relax, and let that person tell his or her story with as much embellishment as possible. As the guide, ask each person to insert themselves into the story so that they are participants. What do they see? How does it sound? What are the smells? What do they feel? Are others talking to them? What are they saying? What is Jesus saying?

Following the exercise, ask members to share their experiences. How did the story become more meaningful because they experienced it? If you are uncomfortable or unfamiliar with guided imagery, I suggest you try Thomas Droege's book titled *The Healing Presence,* published by the Youth and Family Institute of Augsburg College. It is full of guided imagery experiences for you to use.

Servant Event or Retreat. This article shares a way of experiencing God through assisting those who have experienced a tragedy such as the Barneveld tornado. Keep close watch for the events taking place in your community and be ready to gear up to assist. Make sure you ask the why question as you work.

Beyond a doubt, a very powerful tool to talk about experiencing God is through an adventure game experience. Adventure games help us build trust, relationships, community, communication, and problem-solving skills. One does not need to be athletic or young to do adventure activities. For example, have your youth group or family stand on a plastic tarp about 4' x 8'. On the side you start out on write *Life Experiences.* On the side facing down write *Experiencing God in Life.* Try to have no fewer than five or more than ten people on the tarp. Once everyone is on board, ask the group to flip the tarp over without anyone getting off. It usually takes some effort. The more people there are on the tarp, the more difficult it is. If you have a small group, make your tarp smaller. Talk about the experience. What made it difficult? What helped the group be effective? Which side of the tarp do we usually stand on? Do we actively look to find or recognize God in our experiences?

9

Bowed Heads and Folded Hands
The Prayer Proverb

by Thomas Schattauer

> The confessing Christian youth and family community sustains itself in prayer— the prayer of individuals, the prayer of families and small groups, and the prayer of the worshiping assembly. Prayer provides an ongoing link between the energy of youth and the energy of God.

My house shall be called a house of prayer.
Mark 11:17

When the architect I. M. Pei was asked to design the Rock and Roll Hall of Fame in Cleveland, Ohio, he hesitated to accept. How could he build a monument to the legends of rock and a gathering place for the fans of rock if he did not first of all understand this music phenomenon himself? And like most of his generation, he did not. So he took some time—time to listen to some of the classics of rock, time to listen to a daughter who enjoyed this music.

Sometime later, Pei called the planners back and accepted. He stated that now he understood rock music and could begin the design process. The planners were curious to find out what Pei had discovered. So they asked, and he replied, "It's about energy."

Rock music is a cultural icon of youth. It's about energy. In the beat that drives the music, we hear the energy of youth. Young people today and every day are about energy—physical energy, emotional energy, sexual energy, energy of all kinds. Youth is about energy released, energy expressed, energy directed, energy controlled, energy repressed, energy frustrated, energy limited or lacking. It's about energy that powers and propels, energy that overturns and subverts, energy that resists and rebels, energy that gives out and gives up. But it's always about energy.

The life of prayer is also about energy—God's energy. The energy of the one who created the universe; the energy of the cross that destroyed the powers of sin, death, and evil; the energy of the one who draws us together in the communion of the life-giving God: the energy of God—Father, Son, and Holy Spirit.

Annie Dillard is a contemporary writer who tells us about the energy, power, and mystery of God. In her book *Teaching a Stone to Talk,* Dillard writes:

> On the whole, I do not find Christians, outside of the catacombs, sufficiently sensible of conditions. Does anyone have the foggiest idea what sort of power we so blithely invoke? Or, as I suspect, does no one believe a word of it? The churches are children playing on the floor with their chemistry sets, mixing up a batch of TNT to kill a Sunday morning. It is madness to wear ladies' straw hats and velvet hats to church; we should all be wearing crash helmets. Ushers should issue life preservers and signal flares; they should lash us to our pews. For the sleeping God may wake someday and take offense, or the waking God may draw us out to where we can never return.[1]

Young people are often suspicious, like Dillard, of worship that looks like it has more to do with human propriety than with the life-taking, life-risking, life-giving power of God. They also are not impressed, and should not be, with gimmicks that adults design to package God for them. As Dillard suggests a bit further on, prayer takes us "out to the utmost rim of life," where we, young and old alike, encounter the living God and not one who is a mere reflection of ourselves.

Sometimes I fear that we have so domesticated God that the Holy One is little more than a projection of our best and nicest selves writ a bit larger, and all too often we encourage young people to do the same. We sing to a god whom we can know and get close to, not the one who threatens to break out against us. We like to bathe ourselves in the light and glory of God without concern for the fire that will surely consume us and all our projects or, let us hope, refine us for God's own purposes. Are we sufficiently sensible of conditions?

So how do we bring these things together in prayer—the energy of youth and God's energy—in a way that is sensible of conditions? Whatever our age, the basics of prayer are the same.

Whatever our age, prayer permeates life together in the community of faith because it is a way of being in communion with God. The life of prayer begins in baptism, when God claims us in Christ and where the Holy Spirit draws us into the very life of God and into the fellowship of believers. The picture of prayer that derives from baptism is hardly that of an act of human communication directed to a God "out there," but rather an action by which the triune God embraces human speech and action and draws it into communion with the divine life. The practice of prayer with youth would best be established in the communion with God that begins at baptism and continues in the home on a daily basis.

Whatever our age, the practice of prayer is an exercise of relationships: our relationship with God in Christ, our relationships in our home, our relationships within the community of the church, and our relationship to the world around us. Apart from these relationships, our prayers are barren and empty. Without the full set of relationships, our prayers are narrow and unbalanced. There is finally no program for learning prayer other than faithful living within the community of Jesus' disciples, which exists for the life of the world. The practice of prayer with youth, then, must nurture the relationships to God, home, congregation, and world.

Whatever our age, the prayer life of the Christian community embraces a multitude of forms and practices. Prayer is structured and formal; it is also free and spontaneous. The language of prayer draws upon the words and images of Scripture. It employs the rich treasury of speech to God from Christians of every time and place. Prayer involves movement and music as in the public assembly of the church. There is no single way to pray. The practice of prayer with youth should explore, with some intention and purpose, this variety of pattern, language, gesture, sound, and context in Christian prayer.

Whatever our age, the essential movement of prayer and its content involves two things: the recognition of God (Lord God, your mercy is great) and supplication based upon God's faithfulness to us and to the whole creation (Give us a taste of your goodness). These two things are either explicitly stated or presumed by what we say. In prayer we acknowledge the God who was, and is, and is to come, and commend ourselves and all our living together with our world and all its need to this One. We remember and give thanks for all that God has done in creating and redeeming the world, and we beg God for our lives and for our world. We praise and we beseech. And so, the practice of prayer with youth instills the fundamentals of praise and supplication.

Whatever our age, prayer is about listening and discernment: listening to the cry of need from within and without, listening for the movement of the Spirit in our lives and in our world, and discerning how the Spirit's movement relates to the needs of all. Prayer is a kind of correlation of God's purposes with our own sense of need, so that we may come to truly desire and ask for what God intends. The practice of prayer with youth, therefore, involves careful listening to their needs in relation to the vast scope of the world's need, together with genuine discernment about how this need relates both to the mystery of God's purposes and to God's faithfulness to us.

The best instruction in prayer for young people will come from adults who are themselves schooled in the basics of prayer. They will model a practice of prayer that witnesses to the reality of God's love in Jesus Christ, to the work of the Spirit among the people of God, and to the purposes of God for the world. They will invite youth to full participation in the community of faith and its rich and varied prayer life. They will allow young people to contribute their own energy to the practice of prayer and to enjoy the energy of God found among God's praying people.

Suggested Strategies

Caring Conversation. Discuss some of the following with youth and families:
- Share a prayer that you feel was or was not answered.
- Why do people feel a sense of inadequacy when it comes to prayer? How might this be addressed?
- What are the risks in a life that takes prayer seriously?
- What difference does it make to understand prayer not as our effort to connect to a God "out there," but rather as an action prompted by the Holy Spirit?
- How might the energy of youth affect the practice of prayer?

Ritual or Tradition. Ask your pastor to help you identify prayers that fit the rituals of the church year. Use these ritual prayers with youth groups and print them in your church bulletin so they can be used at home.

Family/Youth Group Devotion. Make the point of praying together as a family once a day. Prior to praying, identify that for which you wish to pray. You may want to follow the "sorries, pleases, thank you's" format. For what are you sorry? For what do you want to ask God's help? For what can you give thanks?

Servant Event or Retreat. For a weekend retreat, focus upon prayer—understanding it and strengthening the participants' practice of it. Within the retreat ask different people to offer prayers at different times. (It is helpful to warn them.) There should be some time to concentrate upon the traditional prayer forms as well as more free-form styles. Use this proverb as a point of discussion.

10

Green Hair! Nose Ring! Tattoo! What's Next?!
The Multicultural Proverb

by Elizabeth C. Polanzke

> **All youth ministry is multicultural ministry. Youth cultures represent distinct and different social structures, rules, values, support systems, and guidelines for interaction. Those who work with youth seek to recognize, understand, and respect these varied youth subcultures. This generation of youth needs to feel that they are the driving force behind their own culture and context.**

In the '60s we said, "Make love, not war"; in the '70s we said, "If it feels good, do it"; in the '80s we said, "Greed is good"; and in the '90s we said, "Been there, done that." What does that say about American culture?
Paul Hill

Jocks, punks, moods, hicks, FHA, FFA, bandies, preps, and floaters. I was a floater and sometimes an artsy. That meant I always carried colored pencils (Berol brand) and a sketch pad (with the cover ripped off) in my backpack. The teachers were always more lenient with artsies than some of the other kids because we weren't troublemakers like the hicks, punks, and some jocks. Quite the contrary, we abhorred violence and advocated love and peace for all in our high school. Our study hall teachers would often break their own policies and let us artsies leave study hall in pursuit of an artistic niche outside or in the art wing of the school (a place where administrators rarely trod). I guess you could say we got preferential treatment. We could spend hours reliving a decade we hadn't lived through and plan our next protest march while reading poetry and prose and swapping cassettes by Crosby, Stills, Nash, and Young; the Grateful Dead; and Depeche Mode. That was high school in the '80s.

The things we valued included the environment, anything vogue in the '60s, decent colored pencils, and anyone who was excluded from every other group in school. That's what it took to belong to our group.

But the rules were different for the other groups, and what was valued was different. Each group in school, what some would call clusters, had its own values, way of dressing, language, and, most importantly, a way of being with and for others. Generally, artsies didn't discuss parents (most of us had broken homes, or absentee or abusive parents). When we got together outside of school, entertainment was focused primarily upon sharing music, drawing portraits of each other, and discussing world affairs. That was very unlike the jocks, who attended sports events and valued becoming the homecoming king and queen. It was unlike the punks, who smoked and drank in their free time and in their parents' homes. It was also unlike the hicks, who hung out working on cars. Each cluster was a sort of family. The artsies were family for one another in extreme crises, but primarily because we shared experiences. We didn't judge people by their sexual orientation or promiscuity, because we all considered ourselves misfits and therefore lucky to belong anywhere. In our cluster each of us was free to be who and how we wanted to be. We set the pace. We set the rules, and no one could tell us how to do it differently.

Each youth fits into a cluster that sets the rules, the tastes, the trends, and the outlook of its members. The significant difference today is that the chasm between clusters has grown. The distinctive rules of each cluster have become much more pronounced, making generalizations about youth difficult.

Whether or not your youth dresses like a gang member but is a hippie at heart is determined by his or her cluster and the accepted norms and rules of that cluster. Whether or not a youth drinks alcohol and smokes marijuana is determined by the cluster and its norms. There are few generalities that can be made for all kids from the same neighborhood, or school district.

A youth group in today's day and age will include youth from different clusters and will therefore bear different, and possibly conflicting, values. An effective youth worker/volunteer/parent must be aware that it is a liability if being a Christian means only another set of values and norms. Attempting to impose an external set of norms is difficult. Letting the seed of the gospel take root and grow inside of the youth will go further to raising a Christian than attempting to tear down the norms through which a youth has already found acceptance and comradery. We pray for the Spirit to plant this seed as we are sensitive to, listen to, and relate to these varied youth clusters.

When I think of Christ's disciples, I am reminded that they weren't all fishermen. They came from various walks of life, with certain values and norms based upon religion and socioeconomic classes. Today's clusters are shaped across socioeconomic classes, races, gender, and political/social/religious interests. So, the way the clusters are formed has changed, but like the chosen Twelve, the diversity among Christ's disciples has not. The challenge for you will be to respect the norms of your youth, while nurturing the seed of the gospel and its unique expression found in each youth's cluster.

Suggested Strategies

Caring Conversation. Ask your youth to define the group with which they identify. Ask how they came to be a part of that group and what sets it apart from others.

Ritual or Tradition. Develop a ritual greeting based upon youth culture themes. For example, David Anderson suggests one person says, "In your face" and the other responds, "Full of grace." Another greeting might be that one person says, "Whatever" and the other responds, "Forever." High fives should always be exchanged! Make these phrases new ways of vitally blessing one another. Listen to the language of current youth culture, music, and the movies, and you will hear many possibilities.

Family/Youth Group Devotion. Read Mark 11:15-19. Jesus became angry with a religious culture (cluster) that devalued worship in the temple. Are there youth subcultures that devalue God? How do they do this? Discuss how you can respond. End by praying for those who "diss" the Lord.

Servant Event or Retreat. Provide an opportunity for your youth to visit for a few days with a culture that is completely outside of your own context. If you are a rural church, visit an inner-city or suburban church, and vice versa. Try to pick a time when there will be a lot of people around who can share what their daily lives are like, what they value, what they do in their free time. Include worship as part of this cultural exchange. If you can, have the kids stay in the homes of parishioners. Immerse them and yourself in the different culture as much as possible. Make sure to get together afterwards and process the experience together.

11

It's a Big World Out There!
The Global Proverb

by Winston Persaud

It's a small world!

> **Youth and family ministry is done in a multicultural, global context. It is done in a competitive religious and secular cultural milieu. These larger forces need to be understood if one is to be effective in youth and family ministry.**

I often think of the world in which I grew up. There is a strong nostalgic side to me. Without intending to do so, time and again I ponder my upbringing in Guyana, with its multi-ethnic, multireligious, and complex cultural matrix. My retrospection is inextricably bound up with the question about the kind of world in which our two sons are growing up. My world was unmistakably multi-ethnic and multireligious. We were not middle-class, but we were nurtured in school and church to have middle-class values. Our sons are growing up in a middle-class world, from which they can not and should not be isolated, that is also multicultural, multireligious, and multi-ethnic. In my home, my father, a convert from Hinduism, was a Christian and a member of the Lutheran church, and my mother was a devout Hindu. The tacit understanding in their "arranged" marriage was that their children would be brought up as Christians in the Lutheran church. On the day of baptism of each of our two sons, I kept thinking about the fact that on their mother's side of the family they are in a line of Christians that goes back several centuries. On my side of the family, as far as I can tell, our sons are third-generation Christians.

My family reflects the larger world. Our global world is connected and intertwined in incredible ways, and it increasingly is being connected at a mindboggling pace. In this world, certain basic questions press upon us.

First, is there any foundational truth? Or is truth merely a matter of what each one finds to be meaningful? The question of the truth of the gospel of Jesus Christ is as old as Christianity. It is not a new question. What is new today is that it is being raised in a newly emergent multicultural and multireligious mission field that is not some place overseas. That mission field is very much the North American context in which we live. It is in this "global" context that mission to youth (and to all other age groups) is to be carried out. Youth ask questions about truth. That is part and parcel of being human. This new global world places before us all the pressing challenge of how to witness to the good news of salvation in and through Jesus Christ alone! Christ alone—*solus Christus!*—Luther and the reformers insisted is the gospel.

In our global world there is an unavoidable pressure to view our world of religious plurality as if it were a vast salad bar in which there is an incredible assortment of ingredients for us to make our own salad. Whatever each makes is considered good and tasty. Each one has her or his personal preference. Who is to say that one combination is better than the others? Any judgment is considered totally subjective and therefore true only for the one who made the salad. That is as far as one can go in evaluating the various salad combinations made.

When this analogy is applied to the world of religious plurality, we are faced with three possible options:

1. *All religions are equally valid ways of salvation.* No one is superior to the others. Whatever one finds meaningful is what is true. Here Jesus Christ is one way among several ways of salvation. This is normally referred to as the pluralist model.

2. *All religions find their fulfillment in Jesus Christ, through whom alone is there salvation.* Here there is recognition of partial truth in the other religions. However, the decisive truth is Jesus Christ as the Word become flesh for the salvation of all. If anyone is saved, he or she is saved by Jesus Christ alone. This is called the inclusivist model.

3. *All other religions, apart from Christianity, have no saving content.* To some people, those religions are forms of works righteousness, ways of attempting to work oneself into God's favor and merit God's compassion. In this model, only Jesus Christ saves, and there is no saving reality, however partial and fragmentary, in the other religions. This is the exclusivist model.

Second, how do we transcend the economic arrangement of exploiter and exploited? In this global world, cultural fads come and go, and it is the fads from the Northern Hemisphere that dominate the world. Indeed, we live in a world in which many of the fashionable things we wear, not just tennis shoes and sneakers, are made by people in the Southern Hemisphere, a work force that includes many youth and children who are exploited. Since the fads from the Northern Hemisphere predominate, it is common to see the drive in youth and others in the Southern Hemisphere, as well as those in the Northern Hemisphere, to imitate those fads at any cost. Being connected in the global world has its price, which, in both the short term and the long term, many nations and people cannot afford.

Third, the question of values naturally raises itself. We live in a postmodern world in which there are no absolute values. The certainties we thought we had no longer seem relevant and useful in our highly capricious world. We struggle for a language of values through which we might build bridges across chasms of difference, ignorance, and hostility. In the face of the incredible ease with which we connect across national and other boundaries, it is sobering to consider the reality that we live in a world that is becoming increasingly depersonalized. People are fast becoming things to be used, abused, and disposed of. At the same time, on account of the transnational means of communication, we are made easily aware of such a tragic picture. Such an awareness might prompt us into action to work for justice. Or we may become so overwhelmed by the enormity and complexity of the task that we simply lament, "What's the use; I can't make a difference."

We are overwhelmed by the connection between our consumer tastes, wants, and habits and the obvious exploitation of others who produce those goods and services that we consume. There is such pressure on all of us to create ourselves anew through what we have, possess, and consume. Religious goods are also on sale. What a contrast between this undeniable reality and the gospel of Jesus Christ that in Christ alone, through faith, there is a new creation! God's love is not for sale. It cannot be bought and sold. Anything that is bought or sold as God's unconditional acceptance for Christ's sake is a fake. It is a counterfeit.

Fourth, if our youth are looking for religious foundations—and they are!—then what does the church have to offer? Christ alone! That's the Christian message in a world of competing religious claims. That's the foundation on which we stand and from which we witness to God's incredible compassion and mercy for the world.

Suggested Strategies

Caring Conversation. Have family members discuss where their clothing and shoes were made (look at the tags). Discuss who are involved in the production of these and what the family might know about these people—their culture, their ethnic background, their religious background. How are their lifestyles similar to or different from ours? Is their involvement in the production of the clothing and shoes creative or exploitative?

Ritual or Tradition. Develop a relationship with a sister/brother congregation from another country. Your church leaders can help you establish this connection. Find out as much as you can about your sibling congregation, and write or E-mail them on a monthly basis. Plan a trip to go visit this congregation.

Family/Youth Group Devotion. Center family devotions on Acts 10 and Philippians 2:5-11. Discuss what Paul's and Cornelius's households had in common. What were their differences? How was their encounter with each other a meeting of different religious and cultural worlds?

Servant Event or Retreat. Have youth describe in what ways their communities are diverse religiously, culturally, and ethnically. What do they know about the people in their community who are different? Visit these places and meet the people!

12

We're Here for Ya!
The Church Support Proverb

by JoAnn A. Post

> **The church is a unique place that offers an unconditional welcome to youth and families.**

Come to me, all you that are weary and are carrying heavy burdens, and I will give you rest.
Matthew 11:28

My daughter's ten-year-old friend cannot play in the grade-school orchestra because his parents can't afford the instrument rental fee.

A high school junior lies awake nights worrying about making his wrestling weight; if he weighs even several ounces over guidelines, he can't wrestle. If he can't wrestle, he can't place. If he can't place, no college in the country will offer him a scholarship, and his grades aren't high enough for academic scholarships.

She was excited about the talent contest until she saw and heard the other contestants. "They're so good," she whispered to herself. "I'll never win. I shouldn't even be here."

The counselor asked the grade-schooler when his trouble had started. "When my parents divorced" was the answer. "I'm so afraid I'll make them mad at me like they're mad at each other. What if they leave me, too?"

Every arena of a young person's life requires something extra in order to be part of it: money for equipment rental, physical prowess for competition, talent, brains, maturity beyond their years. Too often that something extra is out of our grasp, making it impossible for the poor child, the pimply teenager, the competitor, the child of a divorced home, to fulfill her or his dreams.

In every arena…but the church.

When our young people enter the doors of the church, all the rules change. In the church it matters not how much money your parents make or whether they live together, what your body looks like, how clear your skin, or how high your GPA. The only thing that matters is that our young people are there, in that place that asks nothing of teenagers but that they keep walking through those doors, day after week after year.

Sometimes this unconditional welcome seems a curse:
- When the confirmation student fails to do memory work: "What are you going to do? Flunk me?"
- When the adolescent Sunday lector stumbles over all the words: "I didn't have time to practice."

We have nothing to hold over their heads, no coercion sufficient to make them perform. We don't grade or punish or pay our young people to do what the church asks. Because this is all we ask: Be there and we'll be there for you. The Spirit will do the rest.

This unconditional welcome is most clearly expressed in our Lutheran understanding of the sacraments of Baptism and Holy Communion. These sacraments, along with careful attention to relevant preaching and being safe and hospitable, are the best and most unique gifts our church has to offer people of all ages. They are simple gifts, unpretentious, offered to young and old, rich and poor, homely and beautiful. These gifts are freely given to the newly born, the nearly dying, the weeping sinner, and the homeless beggar.

But for some reason, the church rarely thinks to uplift and celebrate these gifts to our children and youth. Instead we offer them shallow programming and pizza. Why is it that at the most important points in a child's life we hide our best gifts and offer that which has only fleeting significance? Why not, at the most important points in a child's life, take them to the font and the table?

We teach that Baptism is a sign of God's grace offered to sinners, even before that sinner is able to "respond" in any way to God's love. We teach that it is sufficient for infants to be baptized simply because their parents desire it. We teach that it is sufficient for older persons to be baptized simply because they desire the sacrament. But whether the baptized is a babe-in-arms or a teenager, the church offers encouragement and education at every step. First we teach the parents and sponsors what it means to live as baptized people; later we offer that word to grade school children and teenagers. Ideally, we would continue to teach the baptized life to all in the church, regardless of their age.

On occasion, one hears of youth ministry gone awry as well-meaning youth ministers baptize teenagers in water fountains on retreat or with soda in the church basement (futile efforts to be relevant). While we teach that Baptism is a free gift offered to all, we also encourage the baptized to think and pray carefully about what it means to be baptized, rather than rushing into the water under pressure from peers or the passion of the moment.

We do not demand great acts of devotion before baptizing. Those who minister with youth are able to both welcome young people and incorporate them into the life of faith in a variety of ways:
■ invite the unbaptized to consider receiving the sacrament;
■ live lives as daily dying, newly rising friends and mentors;
■ pray publicly and privately for the gifts of the Spirit;
■ provide safe and hospitable settings.

Once baptized, all are welcome at the Lord's Table. Our church continues to teach that under normal circumstances, the Sacrament of the Altar belongs to those who have become members of Christ's church through Baptism. However, it is not uncommon for young people to receive their first communion without having first been baptized if they worship with a communing friend or find themselves in a group where everyone is receiving the bread and wine but them. No harm is done if such a communion takes place. Rather, such an event is occasion for an invitation to greater involvement in the Christian community and, most significantly, to the font.

Holy Communion requires nothing of the individual but that he or she believes Jesus is truly present in the bread and wine. For the small child, this is indicated by reaching for the elements when they are offered to mother or father. For the grade school child, it is enough for them to say, "This means Jesus loves me." As the child matures in the faith, we hope his or her understanding of and desire for the sacrament matures as well.

Even as we teach that Holy Communion is a free gift, we offer it with love, with teaching, and with prayer. And while our congregational practices must be invitational and accepting, we also must walk carefully between the two extremes of offering the sacrament to "just anybody" and requiring a carefully reasoned, theologically sound statement of faith.

Having said all that, one truth remains: the church is the only place in a young person's life that asks nothing but that she or he be there. With the urging of the Holy Spirit, the love of caring adults and friends, and the gift of time, the young person may choose to do more than simply be there. But first we open the door and invite them into our home, the church.

If we were to adopt a current catchphrase in youth ministry—WWJD? (What Would Jesus Do?)—the answer would be simple. He would welcome children and youth and he would keep them safe. Before sitting at the table with his disciples, Jesus first knelt and washed their feet (John 13). An act of humility, an act of love, an act of kindness for tired, hungry, frightened, undeserving disciples. Just as Jesus invited his disciples to be washed and then to eat, so we humble ourselves before the poor, the athletic, the beautiful, the average, with simple invitations: Come, and be washed. Come, and eat.

Suggested Strategies

Caring Conversation. Ask youth to evaluate whether they feel welcome and safe with your congregation. Interview unchurched youth and find out where they go to be safe and to "lay their burdens down." Ask them if they ever consider a church. Why or why not? Invite youth to help design a welcoming, safe church. For example, perhaps your church can be an after-school homework place for teens.

Ritual or Tradition. Along with recognizing birthdays and wedding anniversaries in the church newsletter, publish members' baptism dates and remember them with a card or phone call. Ask all the children in the congregation to gather around the font for other children's baptisms. Teach them to speak the words of welcome from memory:

> We welcome you into the Lord's family. We receive you as fellow members of the body of Christ, children of the same heavenly Father, and workers with us in the kingdom of God (*Lutheran Book of Worship*, page 125).

Ask the parish pastor to preside at communion on youth retreats or regular youth gatherings; encourage a variety of methods and a great deal of group participation—serve communion to one another, bake your own communion bread, or design the liturgy as a group (a great way to discuss the various parts of the liturgy and why they are present!). Offer age-appropriate educational opportunities about the sacraments at ritual times in a child's or family's life: Baptism, first communion, Affirmation of Baptism, high school graduation, marriage, or the birth of a child.

Family/Youth Group Devotion. Read John 8:1-11. With whom do you identify in this story? Have you ever felt condemned like this woman? Have you ever received forgiveness as Jesus gave? When? For what do you need to be forgiven, unconditionally loved, now? Where do you feel you can go to receive an unconditional welcome?

Servant Event or Retreat. Include children and young people among those who, with the pastor, take communion to the congregation's homebound members; identify families who may choose to serve in this way. Plan a weekend retreat for youth and their families to discuss the sacraments, bake bread, play in water, and share the sacraments together. This can be done with grade school, junior high, or high school young people, or intergenerationally.

13
Let God Build the Body!
The Body of Christ Proverb

by Norma Cook Everist

> Youth are fully gifted and full members of the body of Christ now! Therefore, effective youth and family ministry is a mutual, multi-generational (children, youth, adults, senior citizens) journey emphasizing shared leadership, exploration of the Christian faith, spiritual development, Christian community, life challenges and needs, study of Scripture and the confessions, discovery of personal gifts and abilities, and one's sense of Christian vocation.

Indeed, the body does not consist of one member but of many.
1 Corinthians 12:14

"I'm really kind of glad that Kevin couldn't come on the camping trip. It's easier to have fun without his trying to be the center of attention all the time."

"Hey, how are we going to find something for Jay and Melissa to do at the setup for the Easter breakfast? One's all thumbs and the other whines when asked to do anything."

"I don't think I can be part of that worship service you're planning."
"Why?"
"Well, I'll probably be busy Sunday morning or something." (I don't know why they keep asking; I just don't fit in.)

Many Parts, One Body

The body is made up of not only one part, but many parts. Ministry among youth means ministry among all youth, even when we don't like one another very well. We belong to Christ and, therefore, to one another.

"If the foot would say, 'Because I am not a hand, I do not belong to the body,' that would not make it any less a part of the body," Paul writes in 1 Corinthians (12:15). My hand and foot usually don't carry on conversations like that. Well, maybe they do. When my tooth aches, I'm in agony all over. And if I stub my toe or hit my crazy bone… "If one member suffers, all suffer together with it; if one member is honored, all rejoice together with it" (12:26).

The image of body parts having a conversation may be more valid than the way we actually talk: not saying what we feel; neglecting one person, shunning another, all the while pretending we're best friends. The Body of Christ Proverb rests on the belief that God created us for interdependence, that on our own we'll find all sorts of ways to alienate one another, and ourselves as well. In Christ we, as a falling-apart people, have been literally reassembled into the very body of Christ. The Spirit enables us to believe that and builds up that body, the church.

Ministry among youth needs absolutely every gift of each member of the body. The only thing Sheila can do is make posters? Great! She's needed. All Todd's good for at the car wash is wringing out chamois? No problem! How would we finish the job without him? Jennifer has so many talents that she has a hard time deciding where to go to college? Help her discern her gifts, the need of the world, and her calling. Tom questions his worth? Struggle with him and affirm his great worth among you.

Each gift is necessary. As Paul remarked (Romans 12:6-8), we are differently abled: some diligent, some compassionate, some cheerful, some "tell-it-like-it-is" people. Paul says absolutely, "The eye cannot say to the hand 'I have no need of you.'…On the contrary, the members of the body that seem to be weaker are indispensable" (1 Corinthians 12:21-22). In fact, God has so arranged things that to the "inferior" parts, the parts we think are less respectable, God gives the greatest honor. Imagine that!

For at least 40 years (that tells you when I was in youth group) young people have come home from a youth event with a discovery they eagerly pass along to their elders: Youth are not the church of tomorrow; they are the church of today. The fact that we have to rediscover that truth each year testifies to the difficulty of believing it. All the baptized are full members in the body of Christ. Youth are learners, but not merely in training for service someday. They are already ministers in daily life. The church needs the child, not just to sit at the feet of the pastor telling a children's sermon (for the adults' amusement), but to usher, hand-in-hand with middle-aged Fred, and to sing at the nursing home with Louise, learning old and new songs from one another.

Body building produces strength to work. Community building empowers us to open doors to the world.[1] We need the gifts of all: "Some would be apostles, some prophets, some evangelists, some pastors and teachers, to equip the saints for the work of ministry, for building up the body of Christ" (Ephesians 4:11-12). The Spirit doesn't build up this body just so we can sit around and admire ourselves. God calls youth to take up the challenge to walk around in this world today, to serve, and to be agents of change in a world of danger, death, and doubt.

If community building is at the heart of youth ministry, leadership development is essential to strengthen the muscles. Leadership development takes time, patience, training, support, encouragement.

Youth leaders sometimes abdicate their responsibility in the name of delegation. "It's your event; you decide what you want to do" may come too soon. One step at a time, we learn to walk. So we plan a little, maybe at first even "for" the group—but never "at" them, always listening, listening, listening. Then, as members feel the energy flowing, welcome their ideas, accept their truly volunteering (one can't volunteer for someone else…it's linguistically and practically impossible), and head them toward resources. As people feel steady on their feet, take away the training wheels; they're going on their own. Members learn to work together, rather than being boss or merely competing or sabotaging one another. We are called to be servant leaders who are partners, each mutually accountable to one another as the Spirit builds up the body of Christ.[2] Leadership with youth is best when we move away from being the sage on the stage to a guide by their side.

Here's where the Body of Christ Proverb is a radical idea. The world says, "Forget that church stuff; you need to be in activities where you learn to compete to win, at any cost, in order to make it in this world." But one doesn't hear the elbow saying to the hip, "I'm going to beat you." Body of Christ ministry is relational, not competitive, except in outdoing one another in giving each other honor (Romans 12:9, 10).

Suggested Strategies

Caring Conversation. Check out the three great epistle sections on the variety of gifts and unity in diversity: 1 Corinthians 12; Romans 12; and Ephesians 4. Where do you see yourself? Who else's gifts do you recognize there? Remember that the lists of gifts are not ranked and not closed.

Ritual or Tradition. Nourish the body! Work out by exercising your muscles in an afternoon of work for a parishioner whose body is a bit weary. Feed the body weekly through the intimate eating at the feast of the Eucharist. Chew on the Word yourself devotionally, and try out a new "restaurant," studying together a book of the Bible you've never tasted before. Give it a rest! Be silent; rest your mind and your spirit in meditation. Remember, body building takes more than a day.

Family/Youth Group Devotion. Pray for someone whom you really don't like or who you think doesn't respect you. Pray for a person whose name you can't quite remember, whom you don't see around anymore. God knows the name and will fill your mental blank!

Servant Event or Retreat. No calling is higher or lower than any other. Roles in the body of Christ are to be based on gifts, not gender or race or economics. Together, walk around your neighborhood, surf the Web, or interview some people at work in your community. Explore ways your gifts are needed now…and explore future vocational choices. Tell someone, "I see _____ gifts in you," and point them out. Help make some of their dreaming come true. Help create job opportunities for youth in areas where youth are chronically underemployed.

14

Who Needs a Word Processor When I Have a Typewriter?
The Paradigm Shifts Proverb

by Paul Hill

> **Dramatic change is the norm for society, culture, and the church. Effective youth leaders are attentive to these changes, reflect upon the impact of these changes, and adapt their approaches so that their ministries remain relevant.**

One definition of insanity is doing the same things the same way and expecting different results.
Anonymous

When Moses' father-in-law saw all that he was doing for the people, he said, "What is this that you are doing...?...all the people stand around...."
Exodus 18:14

Pastor Otto Touch was very excited. Marching into his office under the weight of a very large box, he announced, "It has arrived!" The church staff quickly rallied around to see what brought such great excitement to their pastor. He frantically ripped open the box to reveal an electric memory typewriter. "This is what I've been waiting for," he said, "and now I'm up to date!" The staff, the youth minister in particular, rolled their eyes in astonishment. It was 1994.

Poor Pastor Touch. He was operating out of the wrong paradigm—print as primary communication—whereas we are rapidly moving toward a world that communicates, does business, studies, and shares information electronically. The youth minister realized that her senior pastor was not part of the electronic world in which youth live every day. No doubt his VCR had "12:00" flashing all the time.

We all struggle with such shifts in paradigm. Certainly Moses did. In Exodus 18:14 and following we read of Moses, the big-group leader, struggling to become a small-group manager. His paradigm has shifted from "let my people go!" to "let my people get along!" Fortunately, Moses' father-in-law helped him through the transition and, at the same time, introduced the rest of us to the value of small groups.

The history of Sunday school is an illustration of a shift in paradigm. Sunday school is an English invention intended to offer Christian education to children (then often described as "urchins") who had little access to any schooling. The original intent/paradigm of Robert Raikes, the founder of the concept, was outreach ministry to children to "awaken spiritual life in the basest children."[1] The clergy fiercely resisted the idea. One pastor in New York broke into a Sunday school class, screaming, "You imps of Satan, doing the devil's work, I'll have you set in the street."[2] Nevertheless, Sunday school thrived in England and America.

Something has happened over the years with Sunday school. The original purpose of being a tool of outreach to poor children was lost. Yet some congregations are now trying to reclaim the original intent of Sunday school by offering "church school." The primary focus is evangelism and outreach. Church school may take place on any day that works for the people, often Wednesday. The bringing of friends is encouraged, and hospitality is emphasized through such things as the offering of a soup supper for the whole family. Church school has the feel and warmth of a one-room school house rather than the age-segmented industrial classroom.

There are many paradigm shifts taking place. I'd like to identify and briefly comment upon only a few.

1. *We are shifting from a reading and writing culture to a multimedia culture.* Our youth are trilingual at least. They speak at least one verbal language such as Spanish or English. Second, they speak pop culture. This is the language from the worlds of music, fads, television, and consumerism. This pop culture is full of idiosyncratic elements: grunge, alternative, hip-hop, country, and metal, to name a few. Yet there are common threads that loosely bind these elements: MTV, the Top 40 music charts, teen stars and other heartthrobs. Finally, our youth speak computer. Manipulating the electronic world is as familiar to them as riding a bicycle. Trilingual kids move between these three forms of communication effortlessly, guided constantly by the ever-increasing variety and sophistication of media. They are truly the multimedia generation.

Many would assign the Lutheran church the dubious honor of being a left-brain reading and writing church in a right-brain multimedia world. We value words, speeches, organized doctrine, classical and traditional music, and head faith. That which we value primarily goes through our ears. That which our youth understand goes through their eyes, ears, fingertips, and noses. We value content, articulation, and understanding. A multimedia world values entertainment, feelings, and story.

2. *We are shifting from expecting families to support the church to equipping churches to support the family.* The most effective youth ministry takes place in the home, not the youth group. (See the preface, introduction, and Proverb 2.)

This shift flies in the face of the dominant understanding of our church members. Nearly 80% of all Lutherans think that the primary place for faith development is in the congregational setting.[3] Eighty percent of all Lutherans are misinformed: The primary place the Spirit resides and works is IN THE HOME!

The church has a private residence in the home and a public residence in the larger body of Christ evidenced in the local congregation. Our youth and family ministry can help the home be a faith-nurture center and a launching pad for Christian disciples into God's world through the church.

3. *We are shifting from a program-driven youth ministry to a focus on relationship building.* As a camp director I reviewed thousands of camper evaluations.

When asked to identify the most significant part of their camp experience, 95% of the responses answered in a relational way. Campers identified the friends, counselor, or staff members as the key to their experience. We could have saved a lot of money and effort by not developing a program and simply letting the kids hang out with our staff.

Our kids are high tech. They require high touch. Our children have grown up in a tremendously fragmented society. Nearly 60% of all high school seniors in 1991 agreed with the statement "You can't be too careful in dealing with people." This is up from 40% in 1975. Only 20% of 1991 high school seniors agreed with the statement "Most people can be trusted," down from 35% in 1975.[4] Our youth have seen families, churches, schools, heroes, governments, and authority figures fragment, divorce, fall from grace, incompetently operate, or succumb to corruption. Authentic, caring, reliable people willing to build relationships with youth are effective youth ministers.

4. *We are shifting from youth ministry being expert-driven to youth ministry being volunteer-driven.* We need a tidal wave of caring adults to surf with youth, not just a few experts. Let me tell you about one of these caring adults.

Don was not an expert youth worker. Actually he was an iron ore mining executive. He sang in the adult choir of our church. We senior high youth also sang in the adult choir. As I was a rather small, insecure, and unspectacular teen, it would have been easy for Don to overlook my presence at choir. He never did. Every week I got a slug in the arm (a miner's way of showing love) and a "Hey, Paul, how you doing?" from Don. Every time I attended, he took time to talk with me. He always had a warm greeting. Don really knew how to do youth ministry. Don would never consider himself a youth minister. It didn't matter to me. All I know is that I went to choir in part because Don would slug me in the arm.

5. *We are shifting from perceiving youth as incapable to gifted for ministry now.* It was another green hymnal, second setting, Sunday at Holy Trinity Lutheran. Suddenly heads snapped up and eyes strained to see the front of the sanctuary. In the most pure and high voices our elementary choir chanted the assisting minister's part of the liturgy. Our children were leading us in worship! There was not a dry eye in the place.

Jesus viewed youth as gifted for ministry. John 6 reports that a boy with five loaves and two fish facilitated the feeding of the 5,000. Youth have God-given gifts and abilities, though they are young people. Youth are conduits for the Spirit, though they are immature. Youth are in ministry now and need not wait for the future. It is true they need lots of coaching, but coaches stand on the sideline and support their players on the field—they don't replace them.

Youth whom we do not include, engage, and utilize are youth we will never see in church. The single most effective young adult ministry in the Lutheran church is our camping ministry! We give them lousy pay, long hours, hideous living conditions, and work them 20 hours a day, and what do they do? They thank us and beg for more, because they have found in outdoor ministries the chance to share their gifts.

6. *We are moving away from a crisis/problem-solving approach to youth and toward a nurturing and cultivating approach.* The moral of the Humpty Dumpty story

is to put him in an egg carton so he doesn't fall. The Search Institute approach, "Healthy Communities—Healthy Youth,"[5] embraces this paradigm shift. They emphasize building up assets in the lives of youth and have identified 40 of these assets according to categories such as "boundaries and expectations" and "constructive use of time." The presence of these assets makes up a healthy youth ecosystem.

Larger societal paradigm shifts run in conjunction with local changes. Rural, urban, and suburban areas each have their own unique shifts taking place. Effective youth leaders pay close attention to these changes and adapt quickly. The church mantra "but that's not the way we did it before" is a mantra of denial. The ground is shifting; as a result, we are required to take a new stance.

Suggested Strategies

Caring Conversation. As a family or youth group, write down these topics: family, sexual practices, learning styles (or school), church. Feel free to add other topics as well. Discuss what the paradigm was for each of these topics for the adults present and is now for the youth of today. What kinds of things or events have changed the paradigms relating to these categories? How have they changed? Which has changed the least? Why? Which needs to change?

Ritual or Tradition. Paradigm shift 6 speaks of nurturing our children. God has nurtured each of us through our baptism. Do some family research and find out the date and place when and where each member was baptized. Talk about the water and the word and how in the sacrament of Baptism we are washed clean in God's sight. Add these dates to the family calendar of special events. On these baptismal anniversaries celebrate "bath day" with a cake, a reading of the baptismal service, sharing of Matthew 3:13-17, and the singing of "Happy Bath Day to You."

Family/Youth Group Devotion. Review the story of David and Goliath from 1 Samuel 17:24-51. What is David's brother's (Eliab's) reaction to David for leaving the flock? Has anyone in your group or family been reprimanded like this? Do all teens and young adults go through a similar experience of being told they do not belong or "this is not your concern" or "this is for grown-ups"? How do Saul and Goliath react to David's presence?

David was going through a type of paradigm shift as he moved from youth to young adulthood. Is this an easy shift to make? Who or what helps us through this process? What are some of the changes that take place in this shift? How can your church or family be most helpful during this shift?

Servant Event or Retreat. Do a survey of the youth in your church. Ask them to identify by name any and all adults with whom they feel they have a close relationship. Another way to phrase the question would be, "If you were in big trouble, to which adults do you feel you could turn?" Collect the surveys and add up the total number of adults identified. Divide it by the number of surveys and discover the average number of caring relationships these youth feel they have with adults. Plot the number of responses and find the median score. Report your findings to your youth worker, pastor, and church council. Depending upon the results, what can you celebrate or what can you do to enhance adult/youth relationships?

15

Prior Planning Prevents Panic
The Planning Proverb

by Paul Hill

The vision of youth and family ministry is articulated in a specific mission statement that comes to life through goals, strategies, time lines, personnel selection, budgets, and evaluations. Planning emphasizes discovering the gifts God has provided and discerning what God is calling us to do.

We must discern between the immediate and the necessary and do the necessary.
Dwight D. Eisenhower

Dream like a child; plan like an adult.
Unknown

Planning seems to be an unnatural act for human beings. For example, most people do not have personal calendars. I recall once hearing a highly respected seminary president say, "I don't like to do long-range planning; it makes me think too hard." These are words coming from a scholar, theologian, church administrator, and historian! Even major brain power does not free us from the pain of planning.

So, let's just say it and get it over with. Long-range planning is hard work, perhaps the hardest work there is as one develops one's youth and family ministry. It is also the most crucial work that must be done in order to be effective.

The reason long-range planning is difficult is that it forces us to become intentional in our efforts rather than reactive. We must try to anticipate the future (a dubious exercise at any time) rather than live in the present. We are forced to be disciplined in our efforts, which typically is not a common characteristic among those who work with youth. And we must measure our progress, risking that we may discover that we are ineffective. Most important, long-range planning forces us to call into question the traditions, habits, and paradigms out of which we operate. Few people like that kind of scrutiny.

Yet there is a major upside and reason for doing long-range planning. Those who have taken the time and energy to go through a long-range planning process discover that their effectiveness in working with youth increases dramatically. Limited human energy and resources are used most efficiently to the benefit of youth. Perhaps most important, volunteers, youth, and parental involvement increases because everyone knows that their time and energy are not being wasted.

So, where do we begin? I greatly appreciate the leadership Dr. Kennon Callahan has provided in identifying four invitational questions that are pivotal to the planning process:
1. Where are we headed?
2. What kind of future are we building?
3. What are our current strengths, gifts, and competencies?
4. What is God calling us to accomplish in mission?[1]

Using Callahan's approach, what we should ask is, "Where is God calling us to grow to?" whereas most of us ask, "What are we doing wrong?" Callahan's questions set our imaginations in motion; the other question convicts and defeats us.

So, where are we headed in youth and family ministry? In broad terms a number of paradigms and assumptions support our efforts, as any particular ministry will operate within at least a somewhat different paradigm and under a different set of assumptions. However, Proverb 14 may serve as a catalyst for you as you ask, "Where are we headed?"

Callahan's last question is poignant, yet rarely asked: "What is God calling us to accomplish in mission?" Effective long-range planning is a discernment process that asks this question. Certainly it requires our best thinking efforts; lots of research; demographic studies; conversations with parents, youth, and school and civic leaders; and much deliberation. In addition, it asks us to pray, to read the Scriptures, to meditate in silence, and to seek God's voice and guidance. Bible study and devotions are a critical part of the planning process.

Many congregations come at their youth and family ministry from the perspective of "How do we get the kids involved in our church?" This is not the most critical question. The question is, "What is God calling us to do with/for/by our youth in this time and place?" The first question reflects a parochial concern, the second reflects a cosmic perspective.

A long-range plan eventually needs to take a form. There are many outlines available, and I share the following one because it is my favorite format. It is critical that you fill in the blanks in numerical order. For example, a common mistake is made when we begin by asking, "How much money do we have to spend?" and then develop the plan based upon the budget. This is a sure way to shrink your dream. It's easier to cut back on a plan than blow one up. If you have struggled with Callahan's questions first, then it's much easier to fill in the planning outline. Finally, make sure you pray your way through the outline. God is leading you, so listen carefully.

1. The changes taking place are…
2. The constituency we are trying to serve includes…
3. This constituency is most concerned about… (Youth should be involved in the consultation.)
4. God's vision for ministry is… (See Proverb 1—"Faith Formation.")
5. Our specific mission is…
6. The first goal we have in order to do this mission is…
   a. The strategies we have to meet this goal include…
   b. The personnel we will need to meet this goal include…

    c. The facilities we will need to meet this goal include…

    d. The mission money we will need is…

    e. The time line to meet this goal is…

    f. The way we will evaluate our effectiveness includes… (that is, surveys, interviews, numbers, and so forth)

7. The second goal is… (repeat steps a–f for the second, third, and fourth goals.)

Sometimes people get confused between goals and strategies. A goal is the target you are trying to hit. A strategy is the arrow that will hit the target; it is the method by which you will reach the goal. For example, if the goal is to create an exciting new confirmation program, a strategy would be to do community building with the confirmation group.

A final word on planning. No long-range plan is poured in concrete; rather, they are poured in good old gelatin. A long-range plan should be reviewed biannually or more. Its scope should be at least three to five years. As the plan is reviewed, it is fine-tuned, upgraded, and adjusted. This is called a rolling long-range plan. It is flexible yet grounded, adaptable yet rooted. To get started, work with these questions:

1. What plan currently exists (either spoken or unspoken) regarding your youth ministry?
2. What is the process by which this plan came to be?
3. Who owns and advocates for this plan?
4. How is your current plan evaluated?
5. What are the answers to Callahan's four key questions based upon your plan?

    a. Where are we headed?

    b. What kind of future are we building?

    c. What are our current strengths, gifts, and competencies?

    d. What is God calling us to accomplish in mission?

6. Are you satisfied with your plan?
7. Who in your congregation would be good planners that could assist you in designing a new long-range plan? For a long-range planning guide, see Appendix B.

Suggested Strategies

Caring Conversation. As a family or youth group, ask each member to write down her or his goals for the next three months. Share with one another your plans. Why have you chosen these goals? Which is most important? Have you let God shape or influence which goals you have selected?

Ritual or Tradition. Review every three months your family's or youth group's goals, developed in caring conversation. Which goals were met? Which goals were not met? Why? Where have you seen God in reaching these goals? Develop a new set for the next three months!

Family/Youth Group Devotion. Read the story of Jonah together. God had a plan for Jonah. What was it? How did Jonah like God's plan? Did he go along? What is God's plan for you? Join in prayer asking God to help you know God's plan for your life!

Servant Event or Retreat. Take your youth leadership team on a retreat and develop a plan. See Appendix B for a full outline of how to do the planning.

16

W.O.L.F.
The Balanced Ministry Proverb

by Mike Rinehart

> **Effective youth ministry equally incorporates the elements of worship, outreach, learning, and fellowship (W.O.L.F.).**

We need to do more than "Six Flags over Jesus" youth ministry.
Paul Hill

After worship on Sunday morning, Jason, an energetic sixteen-year-old in St. John's youth program, asked the youth committee chair why they couldn't do more "fun" activities. "Look how many people show up when we do something fun! Sixteen kids showed up to go the amusement park, and only five showed up for the Bible study at your house."

At the same time, across Fellowship Hall, a lifelong member of the church was bending the pastor's ear: "Why can't we do confirmation the way we did it when I was a child?" When asked to elaborate further, she talked about how they used to sit in the pastor's study and learn about the Bible. They memorized; they listened; they asked questions. "Are these kids memorizing? I don't understand why they have to do all these servant projects. They should be learning."

The next night at the youth committee meeting, planning was hitting snags. The committee chair was pushing for more "high-appeal" events that would attract the youth, and the pastor was feeling the need for more events with "substance." What they didn't know is that this struggle is a common struggle in many congregations, and for a good reason.

If your church struggles with this tension, fear not. Not only are you in the majority, but your struggle may be a sign of health. In fact, any congregation that does not struggle with this sense of balance may be in danger of creating a one-sided youth program that doesn't offer a full range of ministry to its youth.

A few years ago I was running two programs for junior high youth at my church. One was high content for the highly committed. It provided depth for those who were searching for it. The other was a low-content, sloppy, gross, filled-with-lots-of-surprises program designed to attract new youth and be an entryway to the congregation.

While our numbers were higher for the "sloppy-gross" program, what surprised me were the weekly visitors that were showing up for the high-content program. Moral? How about this: Today's youth are attracted to high-energy fun and games, but deep inside they crave more than just fun and games. They're searching for community—genuine Christian community, complete with trust, love, and conversation on the stuff of their everyday lives (see Proverb 4).

Here's the problem: Youth usually cannot articulate what it is that they want or need, because, like adults, they don't know. This is why the most common approach to planning youth programming always fails. Here it is: The paid or volunteer youth workers gather the youth (and interested adults) for a planning meeting. People who agree to come to such meetings are either well-meaning, innocent, unsuspecting victims, or people with an agenda. In either case it's not a pretty picture.

The leaders ask the youth what they want to do. The kids respond with things like co-ed mud wrestling, a trip to Euro Disney, hide-and-go-seek in the sanctuary, and—my personal favorite—toilet papering the pastor's house. The leaders single-handedly plan the events, and virtually nobody comes. This is a formula the church has used for a very long time. It is usually followed up by a phone conversation like this:
YOUTH PERSON: Hello?
LEADER: Is this Youth Person?
YOUTH PERSON: Yep.
LEADER: Hey, we missed you at mud wrestling on Friday!
YOUTH PERSON: Oh, yeah.
LEADER: Are you sick or anything?
YOUTH PERSON: No, I just don't like mud wrestling very much.
LEADER: But Youth Person, this was your idea!
YOUTH PERSON: Oh well, there was something I had to watch on television.

Fortunately, there is a solution to this dilemma. Just as in our lives we need a good balance between fun stuff and serious stuff, youth programs are the same way. In fact, there are four basic keys to a balanced youth ministry that need attention if a church wishes to keep its program healthy. Think of them like the old four basic food groups: Worship, Outreach, Learning, and Fellowship. W.O.L.F. (FLOW spelled backwards.)

1. *Worship.* Worship is at the center of who we are as the church. The best youth ministries have focused on getting youth to worship through choirs, drama groups, youth services, and so forth. They offer opportunities for youth to worship with youth while off at retreats or by having a devotional time at the beginning or end of youth meetings and events. Strong youth groups pray together and encourage youth to be active in their personal devotions.

2. *Outreach.* In washing the disciples' feet Jesus showed them that the greatest must be least, and that being one of his followers meant being a servant. Reaching out to the world through service, witness, and good stewardship is living the Christian life. Often, serving a needy member of the congregation or community will do more to change the heart than a hundred sermons. After a steady diet of servant projects, youth soon discover that it means a lot more to them than going to the amusement part, and they can have just as much fun.

3. *Learning.* No youth program is complete unless it challenges youth to grow in their understanding of the Bible, the Christian faith, the world they live in, and how these three interrelate. While you may think that the phrase *Bible study* is nearly a death wish in today's youth culture, it is hard to find a single

youth who doesn't want to discuss peace, justice, love, or religious hypocrisy. Youth don't want extra school (which is how they often view the church), but they do want to learn; some just don't know it, because they've equated learning with lectures and tests.

4. *Fellowship.* Of all four parts of a balanced youth program, this is the one that youth will ask for the most. Churches that ignore this do so at their own peril. Adolescence is about relationships. Friends are central to youth. If enduring friendships are not built, youth will gravitate to other places where they can be. Every group, even those built on servant projects, needs time to kick back and just be together. Often the best ministry happens during these unstructured times.

Most churches involve youth in all four areas, but excel in one area while being weak in another. Most youth committees plan youth activities, but rarely ask questions like "How are we teaching stewardship to our youth?" or "How could we emphasize the importance of worship to our high school students?"

A good way to follow the W.O.L.F. model would be to identify your church's strengths and weaknesses. Then capitalize on your strengths. This will bring growth and give you an area to emphasize. Then pray about your weaknesses, looking for ways to improve those parts that need work. This will provide depth to your ministry.

Above all, trust that the one who calls you into ministry will be active in your efforts, providing guidance and direction as you work toward a balanced youth ministry.

Discussion Questions

1. In which areas does your church excel? How could you take greater advantage of these strengths?
2. Are there areas of ministry into which you would like to see youth grow that are not addressed in your activities? (Prayer, stewardship, and so forth.) How could your group grow in these areas?
3. Find out how other churches address the areas that are lacking in your program.
4. Sit down with your pastor, adult leaders, and youth leaders, and ask, "What would an ideal youth ministry at this church look like?"

Suggested Strategies

Caring Conversation. Invite your youth to reflect on their own lives. Do they feel they are balanced? What would they change? Share the W.O.L.F. proverb and ask them to identify how the W.O.L.F. takes shape in their daily, weekly, and monthly activities. Which part would they like more of? Less?

Ritual or Tradition. Start "W.O.L.F.ing" homes, families, and youth groups. Select a season of the church year and W.O.L.F. it. For example: At Easter start greeting other wolves with, "He is risen" (and give them a high five). They respond, "He is risen, indeed." This is worship outreach, learning, and fellowship in one greeting. At Christmas try, "Joy to the world" (with a high five), and the respondent says, "The Lord has come."

Family/Youth Group Devotion. Share the W.O.L.F. proverb in a sermon (or ask your pastor to review it), and invite all families to analyze the balance that exists in their homes. Do they take time to worship, learn from the Bible, reach out, and share fellowship together?

Servant Event or Retreat. Form a task force of youth. Review this proverb; then analyze the last year's activities of your youth ministry. Identify which activities fall in which category of the W.O.L.F. Add up the total and determine how balanced your ministry has been. What areas need strengthening?

17

Invite, Include, Involve!
The Creative Worship Proverb

by Janet Lepp

Effective youth ministry praises God through multidimensional, flexible, and creative public and private worship. All the senses of youth are touched in these worship contexts. It is critical to invite, include, and involve youth in congregational worship.

Every person, including every child, is given gifts to use to enrich the worship of the entire community.
Elizabeth J. Sandell

Youth worship in many ways and in many settings. They worship privately on bike rides or hikes into nature, in quiet moments of thought and prayer, during family devotions, and in the privacy of their rooms. (My daughter worships in her room while listening to Christian rock music that is turned up *loud*.) They worship publicly at church camp, during confirmation classes, at evening youth events, at conventions, and with their congregation on Sunday mornings. They worship at any time when caught ready to experience the awe of God. Young people, even very young children, are able to worship and experience the presence of God. They need to be part of a worshiping Christian community and be given opportunities to acknowledge the saving power of Jesus Christ. They need a chance to explore what it means to be a Christian in our world. Unfortunately, many young people are bored by their congregation's worship and choose not to attend public worship or begrudgingly attend to appease their parents. What can be done to help youth participate more in congregational worship?

Worship Leadership

Youth are dramatically more enthusiastic about congregational worship when they participate in leadership roles, either individually or as a group. Youth leadership in a congregation's worship life should not be delegated to certain Sundays or certain parts of the worship service, because then youth get the message that they are not real members of the worshiping community. A better model is to have adults and youth work together to plan, lead, and participate in worship. If we take seriously the partnership of all believers, we will find ways to partner with all members of the congregation, including the youth.

Youth choirs hold a special place in helping young people develop worship leadership skills. Because choirs set aside time to rehearse, the members can be prepared to present scripture-based musical anthems, lead hymn singing, be the cantors, read the lessons, usher, create or design bulletin covers, prepare communion, or write and say prayers. During youth choir practices, adults set aside the time to work together with youth to prepare for worship.

Individuals not in choirs should also have the opportunity to contribute to worship leadership. There are endless ways in which a young person can contribute to worship. Often, however, youth are nervous about agreeing to serve in a worship leadership capacity. Here are the steps that I use when I invite, include, and involve youth as participants in worship:

1. *Compile a talent list.* I have a "talent list" notebook in which I have listed each young person along with his or her special talents, activities, likes and dislikes, and past leadership participation. I include as many specific details as possible so that a realistic judgment can be made about ways that a youth will be able to participate. It is extremely necessary for a young man or woman to be asked to contribute in ways in which he or she is capable of achieving.

2. *Ask specifically.* I then ask them to contribute a specific, achievable task, such as reading a lesson on a certain Sunday, designing a bulletin cover for the Christmas program, singing the kyrie, or providing the prelude.

3. *Prepare and practice.* After the young person accepts the invitation, I work with him or her. There is nothing more frightening to anyone than to be expected to perform a task and to be uncertain about the procedure. Certainly worship of our God deserves the finest efforts any of us can provide. That effort includes practice and preparation.

4. *Pray.* I pray with the young person so that the Holy Spirit will guide us in leading others in their worship.

5. *Show appreciation.* After the worship is over, I show appreciation, orally and with a written note. I thank them and tell them how their leadership has helped the congregation's worship or my personal worship.

Worship Language and Music

In addition to participation in a leadership role, youth tend to be more interested in worship if they understand the worship language. Words such as *kyrie, sanctification, postcommunion canticle,* and even *Alleluia* or *Hosanna* may have no meaning for them. They may make no connection to parament colors and symbols that assist worshipers by telling the story of Jesus' life. Young people need help to know better what happens in worship. The meanings of the words of faith, the liturgy, Christian symbols, and the church year calendar can be taught during Sunday school, in youth choirs, and in children's sermons. Using the traditional words the faithful have used through the ages creates a powerful witness of identity and Christian unity.

Careful consideration of the language of the society must also be made to ensure that the words are inclusive and reflect the current definitions, always keeping in mind the integrity of the message.

Tension often exists in congregations over what style of music to use, and the youth somehow get thrown into that debate. It is false to assume that if a certain style of music is used in church, youth attendance at worship services will automatically increase over the long term. Youth today have had exposure to all types of music and are as diverse in their musical tastes as adults are. However, it is equally false to assume that youth will tolerate the same old stuff over and over again. Keeping the best of the tradition while adding the new seems to work well in many churches.

The wise selection of music is important so that worship is truly a time when God is honored and praised. Music has the potential to carry the message of God's salvation in very powerful ways. The combination of rhythm, melody, and words allows the messages conveyed in the music to work their way into a person's memory and stay in the mind and heart for a long time. The songs of faith that even very young children learn are capable of shaping that person's theology for life.

Worship Using All the Senses

Youth are also more interested in worship if the service stimulates all the senses in a variety of ways. To really hear the message, young people use their senses of hearing, seeing, touching, and smelling, as well as body movement. They are sensitive to time and have attention spans that often require special care with regard to pacing.

Recently our youth choir participated in worship and helped lead several segments of the service. They sang, read scripture lessons and prayers, and played the choir chimes and the drums. They listened to prayers and the sermon and the music played on the organ. They watched one another, the pastor who held their attention with visuals during the sermon, the acolyte, the ushers, and the flute soloist. They looked at the flowers and the banner. They moved during the peace, swayed during their musical anthem, and walked to take communion. They smelled the candles and the grape juice. They tasted and touched the communion elements. They held their hymnals, shook hands with one another, and picked up their choir chimes. Because they had just studied the seasons of the church year during choir practice, they noticed the designs of the windows, the paraments, and the bulletin cover. All of the senses combined as they worshiped God and celebrated being together.

In Christ

In worship, God is the center and subject of all we do—that mysterious, awesome, creating, and loving triune God! When Christians worship, we combine all of our individual selves in the one body of Christ. Each person brings special talents and gifts, preferences and needs, and combines them with others in offering to our God. Public worship can have the power to bring differing individuals with various interests and strengths into a setting where we can connect with one another, and in that connecting we become individually and communally stronger as the church in the world, capable of loving our neighbors. Let's invite and assist our youth to be one with us in Christ by inviting, including, and involving them in worship.

Suggested Strategies

Caring Conversation. Bring a group of adults and youth together and ask them each to identify a piece of music or song that is particularly meaningful. What memories and feelings does this music awaken? Is there worship music that has any particular power and meaning to the group? What is it? Why?

Ritual or Tradition. In your family find out what each family member's favorite worship song is. To what part of the church year does it connect? (For example, "Joy to the World" connects to Christmas.) Throughout the church year, sing together these songs at home and in the car, and request them at church.

Family/Youth Group Devotion. As a family or youth group, listen to a popular song. What do the words say and what messages are given? Many songs today give a message of despair and hopelessness; other songs may hold messages disrespectful of human life. Now think of what the Bible says about the value of life and of humanity. (Possibilities might include John 3:16; 1 Corinthians 13; Romans 3:21-24; Romans 8:31-39; Romans 8; Luke 10: 25-37.) Compare the messages of the popular song with the messages of the Bible.

Servant Event or Retreat. Many families and youth groups go caroling and visit homebound people at Christmas. How about also doing this at other times of the year? Shut-ins and people in nursing homes and other care centers often yearn to hear hymns and other songs of faith, especially the ones they remember from their past. Prepare several songs that are congregational favorites or those known to be favorites of those being visited, and have fun sharing them with those you visit. Be sure to allow time after the music to talk with them.

18
Body Guard
The Justice Proverb

by Anne Helmke

Children and youth are the most vulnerable members of society. Clergy and staff, congregational leaders and members, and parents and youth must be advocates of youth and willing to speak with and in behalf of youth. Establishing places of justice, fairness, and safety are critical advocacy steps.

And what does the Lord require of you but to do justice, and to love kindness, and to walk humbly with your God?
Micah 6:8

Justice. Righteousness. Generally speaking, *justice* and *righteousness* have different definitions, but both are related to the same the Hebrew word, *sedaqah*. The biblical concept of sedaqah encompasses some of what both of these English words mean, and therefore they are related. This provides the first insight into the Justice Proverb.

It is not uncommon to hear a young person (or an adult) say, "It's not fair!" Whether that young person is referring to a parental or teacher decision or to a perceived unbalanced peer privilege, fairness and rights seem to be core concepts in his or her functioning definition of justice. As poor Job could well tell us, justice does not always appear fair. Justice is not always a reward for the goodness of a person. And it is not always a due punishment for wrongdoing. If this were true, grace and forgiveness and mercy would not have meaning.

The definition of God's justice holds more meaning than reward and punishment. God's justice is restorative. And so enters justice's twin, righteousness (doing what one is supposed to do), in the making of sedaqah. As truth seekers and justice bearers of the past have discovered, sedaqah is always relational, but not always rational (at least not rational in human terms). Justice understood within this larger definition to include righteousness always seeks to mend and reconcile the relationships between inner and outer individual self, between ourselves and others (both one-on-one and corporate), between humanity and the rest of creation, and between human beings and the creator. Justice is the righting of relationship.

The younger generation can find itself overwhelmed by even considering the mending of all the broken, unjust relationships that surround them. Many believe that they will not even survive their twenty-first birthdays! Their world may appear dark and hopeless. Violent behavior, drugs, and alcohol (to name a few expressions) can no longer be excused as pubescent behavior. These mutant behaviors of young people can no longer be excused as the result of dysfunctional family and life situations. These may all be contributing factors to destructive behavior, but as people of faith we need to begin hearing these actions as expressions of pain—cries of hopelessness and oppression. This is the second insight into the Justice Proverb.

Before the exodus, God heard the Israelites' cry of oppression and then responded by setting them free! Many solution makers respond to the cries of the younger generation today by wanting to fix or punish the behavior instead of hearing the pain. More than likely the response to watching unacceptable behavior and the response to hearing a young person's struggle would be two entirely different actions. Once perceptions move from watching to true hearing, a relationship begins to develop—reward and punishment is replaced with compassion and love. And when we have someone to walk with us in our struggle (as *compassion* implies), and when that someone authentically exhibits that what happens to us matters to him or her, then our steps become somewhat freer, the oppressive darkness of life situations is cracked open with hope-filled light, and the process of liberation has begun!

The third insight into the Justice Proverb relates to compassion and love. This is what was so extraordinary about Jesus' ministry and model. His court of justice did not operate with rewards and punishments, nor did it appeal to rights. If it had, he would have never associated with prostitutes and tax collectors—or even engaged in dialogue with hypocritical faith leadership. He ate, he touched, and he talked with all people because he loved them! Jesus lived by the rules he preached—love God, love neighbor, love even enemies. That's everyone! His justice was relational, radical, but not rational.

God's justice is always about loving the other—whoever that may be—but it doesn't always mean seeing the same way as the other, or even liking the other. However, *love* is one of the words that has lost its meaning and is often tossed away like a used tissue in today's consumer-oriented world. The choice to love moves past and deeper than the feelings of like and hate. And if chemistry has anything to do with love, it is the unique and reactive combination of respect for the other's life and an authentic search for the truth that is God-given in the other's life.

The tricky part of the justice proverb is not so much in believing in its truth or even in describing justice. What's tricky is how the words of justice become living action. What does justice look like, especially in the lives of the younger generation?

Justice is the righting of relationship. When listening, teaching, or guiding a younger person, it is helpful to keep this discerning question in mind: What relationship(s) is in need of righting, of restoration? This question helps sort out the issues at hand. Whether the brokenness or anger is between the young person and parent, peers, an institution, God, or whatever, this question will help to clarify how to reach justice and when there is an authentic injustice.

Justice is about hearing the cries of hopelessness and oppression. This hearing runs in at least two directions. As someone who shares ministry with young people, taking time to truly hear their cries as pain—or providing ways and places where their cries might be better heard (advocacy)—are critical and crucial justice steps. This can be enacted anywhere—one-on-one on a nearby step; opening up ways that young people might speak and serve at solution-making tables; or in a local television studio (religious or public) where an open forum on pertinent issues might be designed, produced, and led by young people. The ways of hearing and advocacy are limited only by our imaginations!

And, as with all the insights and disciplines of nonviolent justice, young people can learn to hear the cries of others who seek justice.

Justice is created through acts of authentic compassion and love. When one person truly says to another (in words or through actions), "What happens in your life matters to me," the way of justice has begun. Suddenly, all things change as the cry is heard and is greeted by compassionate love. Many adults are grasping for solutions in response to this turbulent world of the young. Mentoring and conflict-resolution programs in schools and churches are making significant strides. However, grand-plan programs are only as effective as the simplest portion. When asked by adults, "What can I do?" I respond with "Find one young person—listen, be with them, love them as Jesus loves you, and authentically show them that what happens to them matters to you." That's compassion and love!

Remember, injustice breeds a sense of insignificance that can grow into despair and blossom into hopelessness; but if the tables are turned out of the deep love of another's soul, significance replaces insignificance, which fosters promise and provides hope where justice might take root!

Suggested Strategies

Caring Conversation. Invite a group of youth and elders to a storytelling time. Stories to be shared around the table can be personal or known by the participants and should respond to this question: Has anything ever happened to you or someone you know that does not seem fair or is unjust—something that really makes you angry?!…and why? What would have to happen in order for justice to occur? How could that be accomplished?

Ritual or Tradition. Prayer vigils have been a tradition within Christianity since the early church. Vigils may vary in the size of those gathered together, location, content, and so forth, but here are a few examples of types you may wish to hold:

■ Symbolic vigils may be held in a church, home, or wherever continuing injustice or violence might occur (for example, at a children's hospital where young people enter every week because of abuse, a homeless shelter, a historic battle site).

■ Responsive vigils are held in response to a recent occurrence or concern of the community (for example, site of a recent shooting or other act of violence, someone's home that has experienced a great loss or injustice).

■ Virtual vigils are organized around a specific moment in time, and people pray wherever they are at that given moment (for example, All Hallow's Eve, World Day of Peace, January 1st).

In all cases, let simplicity be your guide. Ask people, young and old, to bring candles, and then let the prayers and possible songs flow freely. Prayer vigils provide a voice to the pain and injustice, both to God and to others. It can be a critical step toward advocacy and healing.

Family/Youth Group Devotion. Ask everyone to write a prayer about something they would like to see happen or accomplished and for guidance in that. Have them fold their papers and place them at Psalm 85 in their own Bibles or in one common Bible. Before closing the Bible, agree on a future date to review the prayers. Read Psalm 85 in closing and commitment. At the agreed-upon date, review the prayed-over desires and consider repeating the above steps.

Servant Event or Retreat. M. K. Gandhi believed that anger worked much like electricity: it could burn down an entire village, or if channeled constructively, it could light the entire village. Have conversation participants brainstorm ways to constructively channel their anger. Ask them to answer these questions: What if we/I did this/that? How might these ideas better light our/my life and community? What would be our/my first step(s)? Could these ideas be added to our/my prayer(s) above?

19

Give Them a Purpose
The Peer Ministry Proverb

by Lyle M. Griner

To the world you may be nobody, but to somebody you may be the world. — Unknown

"Truly I tell you, just as you did it to one of the least of these who are members of my family, you did it to me."
Matthew 25:40

Four words are necessary for successful high school ministry: *Give them a purpose.* While many churches are still trying to create a bigger and better hayride—thinking that entertainment will rebuild the slacking youth program, what high school youth need to be interested and involved is *purpose!* Most youth already are overly saturated with a mixed bag of social life, pressures to achieve in school, holding down a job, changing family relationships, and any number of extra-curricular activities. As a consequence, many youth don't attend church programs—not because they think the church is bad, but because their time already is so highly committed. If youth are going to be at the church, they have to feel that time spent there is worthwhile: it must have purpose. For many high school youth, a relevant and attractive purpose is to become even better equipped for what they often already do best—be a friend. Peer Ministry accomplishes that purpose by giving youth the skills needed to help when friends are struggling.

Ask any group of youth to raise hands if they know somebody whose family is changing due to a divorce or separation, who is depressed or suicidal, who is struggling with an eating disorder, who is concerned about self-worth, who has ever been abused, who has strife due to one of many sexual issues, who has been involved in violent behaviors, or who worries about everyday relationships. The list of social issues can go on and the hands will continue to go up. Youth know other youth who are hurting. And they want to help.

Peer Ministry is the good Samaritan story (Luke 10) in action. Youth develop skills that help them take action to help others. The best definition for Peer Ministry is adapted from Barbara Varenhorst, Ph.D., Pastor Rick Schowalter, Ph.D., and me: "Peer Ministry is a way of life. It is a habitual practice of doing good unto the least of these my brothers and sisters to the glory of God. Peer Ministry is mutual ministry in that the peer minister expects to learn as well as teach, expects to receive as well as give, expects to be loved and cared for as well as to be loving and caring. Peer ministers grow in the midst of mutual sharing of both their strengths and weaknesses—regardless of age, wisdom, knowledge, authority, or expertise."

- Loves God.
- Loves his or her neighbor as himself or herself.
- Is warm, genuine, and empathetic.
- Helps clarify concerns and values.
- Listens for the meaning behind the words.
- Explores alternatives and consequences.
- Asks open and feeling level questions.
- Makes observations and checks assumptions.
- Realizes that not all problems can be solved.
- Realizes that not all people want to be helped.
- Knows when and how to refer someone to more skilled help.
- Welcomes outsiders into his or her groups.
- Prays for others and their needs.

Quality Training in Caring Skills

While many youth ministry resources use words in their titles like *quick, easy, instant, no preparation*, and so on, Peer Ministry takes skill and time. It is not a program; it is a process. Skills first are learned; next are practiced; then are tried, refined, and tried again; and over a period of time become part of one's life. These skills include listening, encouraging openness with questions, welcoming a stranger, decision-making, modeling positive values, respecting confidentiality, and sharing faith. Peer Ministry is only as successful as the foundation on which it is built and the commitment of those who implement it. That requires dedicated and trained adult facilitators.

An adult who attends facilitator training not only gains expertise in teaching youth to be peer ministers, but also gains the opportunity to discover and work on his or her own faith and skills. Acting on that opportunity is extremely important: youth know when a facilitator doesn't practice what she or he preaches! The adult facilitator's faith and life need to model what is taught. One young girl told me, "I understood Peer Ministry after I spent time talking about one of my concerns with Rob (her adult facilitator) after a training session."

Growth in Christian Faith and Values

As a youth and family minister, I constantly struggle with how to better communicate the good news of Christ and the practice of faith and values. For example, I can teach creative fun and interactive lessons on the Lord's Prayer, but early on, I realized that my brilliant ability to teach did not persuade youth to pray. I looked around. Where did youth see models of people who prayed? It was not something that happened in most homes, aside from a few who said a memorized prayer at meals. For many, the only models of people who prayed were me and the pastor. But we were paid to pray. I'm not sure that we counted. How were youth going to learn how to pray and build other faith-filled habits that would lead them through life?

An answer to that question came after I trained a group of high school youth in Peer Ministry. Many of the youth begin to pray, read the Bible, discuss life and faith issues, and attend worship more often. They begin to lead small group discussions and pray with other youth. Suddenly youth saw real-life people—peers—who actually prayed! And they weren't paid to do it.

These peer ministers not only led small group discussions, but they assisted on camps and retreats, they welcomed anyone and everyone who joined us, they helped individuals cope with the various issues that life dealt, and they guided other youth to seek help when needed. I had the answer to my question: Prayer and faith practices are best taught through the modeling of people who live them.

Passionate Service to Others

The word *training* assumes that action will follow. Churches have found various ways for peer ministers to put their training into action. Some become a mentor to one other person, some become part of a team that leads a particular program, others use their skills with people they meet everyday.

Following are examples of how various churches have put their peer ministers into service.

Once a week at **First Community Church,** 80 to 100 high school youth come together for a campfire-style opening complete with skits, good humor, sing-alongs, and a short introduction. After this opening, small discussion groups, each led by a couple of youth from the Peer Ministry team, spread throughout the church building for caring conversations.

Peer 19 is a collection of small rural churches that all share a common school district, through which Highway 19 runs. Together, they have a Peer Ministry group of 20 youth. These youth meet weekly to discuss what is going on in their community and how they can reach out to those who are hurting.

St. Andrew's is in a community that has a history of teen suicide. Its peer ministers know how to refer youth to adults in their schools, churches, and communities. As leaders for church and community youth events, they listen to their classmates, friends, and neighbors. If they detect situations that need to be dealt with, they offer to go with the person to a caring adult who can help the person in need find appropriate counseling.

St. John's peer ministers go on all the confirmation retreats and camps. They lead the campfires, contribute to presentations, and lead all the small group discussions. It is in these small group conversations about faith and life issues that relationships are built.

Faith Church's Peer Ministry group meets Sunday mornings at 7:30. Each one is assigned to meet weekly with three 9th grade youth as part of the confirmation class time. The peer ministers also send birthday cards, call their assignees periodically, and invite them to church events.

Zion's peer ministers train at a summer camp to be able to help lead an evening program for upper elementary children. During this program they involve the children in interactive dramas, participate with them in games and singing, and create a caring, safe atmosphere.

One **county corrections department** in Minnesota now encourages churches in the county to develop Peer Ministry groups that will welcome troubled youth into their congregation's youth programs. While the corrections department has excellent programs, it realized that youth coming out of those programs continued to need support from other youth, and the best came from church youth groups.

Steps to Get Started

Step 1: Put together a Peer Ministry vision. Focus your vision on the ministry that will be most significant for peer ministers in your church. People need to know the desired results before they start.

Step 2: Train Adult Facilitators. Dedicated adults need to be trained to facilitate the program and supervise the service. Both the dedication and the training are a necessity because trained adult facilitators will train interested and/or selected high school youth in Peer Ministry.

A Peer Minister Does Not ...

- Tell people what to do.
- Bandage problems with cheap sympathy.
- Talk mainly about himself or herself.
- Encourage dependency.
- Put people down.
- Gossip.
- Act as if he or she is superior to others.
- Expect all problems to be solved easily.
- Work with problems beyond his or her capabilities.
- Judge others.

Peer Ministry Consists of Three Elements

1. Quality training in caring skills.
2. Growth in faith and values.
3. Christian service to other people.

Step 3: Inviting Participants. Youth invited to participate should have interest in the program and have demonstrated (through actions or attitude) their care for others. Churches often strive for a diverse group that includes active and inactive youth group members who represent different schools, friendship groups, and cultural backgrounds. This insures that the group's service and outreach will be to more than just the existing youth group.

Step 4: Training. Training may be done once a week, during a retreat, or as a combination of both. Youth will learn best if they have time to learn each new skill, practice that skill in their own life settings, and then discuss how things went with the trained facilitator and the other peer ministers in training.

Step 5: Supervision of Mission. After youth are trained, they need opportunities to implement what they have learned according to the church's mission. The youth should continue to meet regularly with an adult facilitator to evaluate how things are going and for support and ongoing training.

Step 6: Give Them a Purpose. Peer Ministry works because it is about what is most important to youth: their friendships and their faith. Youth discover that Peer Ministry is about living a life that offers hope to others. Youth discover that they are important to the church of today. Youth discover a path of calling that leads to the habitual practice of caring and modeling a life of faith.

Suggested Strategies

Caring Conversation. In the midst of training, have adult facilitators give youth training to be peer ministers an assignment that asks them to practice the skills they are learning in conversations at home, at school, and in other aspects of their daily lives. When the group meets again, ask the youth to share portions of their conversations. Use what is shared about the conversations as a basis for talking about the impact and importance of Peer Ministry.

Family/Youth Group Discussion. Invite family members and others from the church to participate together in a demonstration of Peer Ministry. Peer ministers create a welcoming atmosphere and plan to share their stories and what they have learned, keeping confidentiality in mind, of course. To demonstrate some of the skills peer ministers have learned, they could lead a conversation with one of the parents. Key in on a basic skill demonstrated in the conversation and then let everyone choose a partner with whom they can practice that skill. End by inviting everyone present to pray for the everyday ministry of caring.

Ritual or Tradition. One important way to recognize the commitment and service that peer ministers offer the congregation and community is to commission them for mission at a formal commissioning service during worship at the end of their training. Have the pastoral staff recognize the commitment of the youth and encourage their ministry. Post a picture of the peer ministers and their names. It is great for younger students, too—they can aspire to be that kind of caring person.

Servant Event or Retreat. Visit a nursing home, or other group facility where peer ministers can pair up with residents for conversation. Meet beforehand with the facility's staff to learn about how to approach and care for the residents. Meet afterwards to discuss how the group's training applied.

For Resources, Adult Facilitator Training, Youth Retreats, Camps, and Support

National Peer Ministry Center
Youth and Family Institute
of Augsburg College
Campus Box #70
2211 Riverside Ave.
Minneapolis, MN 55454-1351

(612) 330-1598
Fax: (612) 330-1595
E-mail: PeerMin@augsburg.edu

Visit the web site of the Youth and Family Institute of Augsburg College for updates.
www.augsburg.edu/ayfi

20

Road Trip!
The Events Proverb

by Ralph Yernberg

Effective youth ministry incorporates significant retreat, camp, and servant experiences into the programmatic offerings.

He said, "Go out and stand on the mountain before the Lord, for the Lord is about to pass by."
1 Kings 19:11

That camping and retreat experiences serve to foster healthy youth and family ministry is an established fact. It even has been argued that it is impossible to have a strong youth program in a congregational setting unless camping and retreat ministries are found at its core. The history of this partnership goes back to the turn of the century, when pastors and lay leaders first began to take youth to private cottages for youth meetings or rented facilities for church youth camps. In more recent days, camps have responded by offering a plethora of outdoor adventures from backpacking in some of the more pristine areas of the country to sponsoring service retreats to rock climbing, kayaking, sea surfing, canoeing, and much, much more!

Statistics also show that youth are participating in these exciting opportunities in record numbers. However, it might be argued that youth leaders have taken outdoor ministries for granted in the sense that few leaders have stopped to ask why it works. What is the philosophy of camp and retreat programming that makes it such an effective tool for youth ministry? And why do we affirm its importance in the program of every church?

Reduce camp and retreat ministry down to the basics and you will find four simple themes. First, it is a time of community. The camp and retreat environment is dedicated to building relationships through shared experiences. Whether that experience be hiking, discussing the Bible, playing a game, or singing at a campfire, it is done together. No one goes off on his or her own; each activity of the experience contributes to the corporate nature of the community.

Second, the event is shaped by Scripture. Church camp and retreat ministry has as a basis an encounter with God's Word. That Word shapes and clarifies the event. Most of the time, significant activities of the camp week or high adventure trip are designed around a particular Bible text. This fundamental characteristic shapes the conversation of the event.

Third, a camp or retreat offers each participant an opportunity to enjoy a youth-oriented ritual experience. Youth often will remember participation in a meaningful campfire, the routine of daily morning worship, or the personal time spent in a daily solitude experience. These are rituals upon which youth campers build a sense of personal devotion and spirituality that becomes part of a new behavior of the future.

Finally, camp and retreat ministry offers youth a chance to consider their vocational and avocational interests. Youth are given time and opportunities to make simple (and perhaps complex) choices about what they hope their lives will include. Such choices are as simple as deciding it is in our best interest to recycle, discovering that outdoor camping makes a great hobby, making plans to serve as a future camp counselor, or developing a sense that the Christian church is a good place to belong.

Any program that helps develop community is shaped by the gospel, provides plenty of patterns that foster personal growth and devotion to Christ, and helps us make important choices in life has to be considered an essential principle of youth ministry. That is why so much support in the church is directed toward the effective programs offered through camps and retreats. Ask around and you will discover that the best youth programs are high on offering camp and retreat programs for their participants.

Suggested Strategies

Caring Conversation. Gather your youth together with parents and senior citizens. Invite each person to talk about a significant camp, retreat, or other outing in which she or he has participated. What made the event significant?

Ritual or Tradition. Encourage all families to do an annual retreat. Help them realize the importance of establishing such a pattern for their family. This retreat could include vacation plans, but would incorporate a spiritual emphasis as well (see Proverb 16 for suggestions on balancing the time together).

Family/Youth Group. Devotion: Jesus always seemed to be trying to go on a retreat. He needed to get away from the crowds. Read Luke 4:1-12; Matthew 26:36-45; and Matthew 17:1-13 for examples of Jesus on retreats. To which of these stories do you most relate? Why? Do you get enough retreat time? How can you incorporate retreats into your life?

Servant Event or Retreat. Plan an intergenerational summer week and utilize one of the many camps of the Evangelical Lutheran Church in America. See the ELCA national outdoor ministries guidebooks for some good ideas!

21

Holy-istic!
The Healthy Communities Proverb

by Kelly Chatman

> **Youth are served and supported effectively when the various systems of which they are a part work cooperatively to benefit youth. These systems include families, schools, churches, extracurricular programs, police, courts, and businesses. These systems make up the civil structures of God's creation and are intended to nurture our youth to mature, healthy adulthood.**

All Kids Are Our Kids
Peter L. Benson

Youth and family ministry is the sharing of the organic stuff that makes society function and the church a faith-formation incubator. Youth and family ministry may be described as the first and an ongoing step in the lifelong pathway toward establishing healthy congregations, schools, and communities. A challenge we face in the church is to recognize and communicate the kind of power and influence given by God to shape the lives of youth and the systems that serve them. Effective youth and family ministry empowers youth, as well as the entire community through which youth develop identity, faith, and emotional and spiritual character.

Imagine classrooms and school yards where youth feel safe and secure to grow and neighborhoods of would-be gang members as places of harmony. Imagine families where children and adults eat together. The church remains the one institution with the power and influence to communicate such a reality. In order for such visioning to become reality, today's youth need to experience a radical church where the power and influence of the gospel is organic to the peer group, home, school, and community.

A friend reminded me of an experience we shared as children, a summer adventure that began with borrowing jelly jars from our parents' kitchens. We punctured small holes in the metal lids of the jars. Then we began the wild quest to capture bumblebees. Once we caught a bumblebee, we immediately put it into the jar and quickly shut the lid back on the jar. We then watched the bee as it attempted to escape from the jar. I didn't realize this at the time, but I have grown to learn that if we had left the lid on the jar for only a couple of hours, the bees would have given up hope, accepted the limitation of their confinement, and lived the remainder of their lives in the jar. After just a couple of hours with the lid on, even if the cover were taken off the jar, they would remain in the jar until they died.

Much like the bees confined to the jar, many youth today are confined to gangs, drugs, violence, poverty, and abuse. Far too many youth have yet to experience life from beyond the confines of the jar. As a result, they often react much like the bees: after even a short confinement, they no longer believe they can move out of that confinement, even when an opening is provided.

In Luke 3:4-6 we hear John the Baptist's cry from the wilderness: "Prepare the way of the Lord...all flesh shall see the salvation of God." One of the greatest challenges confronting youth ministry today is to answer the question, How are we to minister in a world where youth have been left to live their lives from within a jar? Youth frequently experience life as hostages to pressures such as violence, consumerism, eating disorders, racism, and drug and alcohol abuse. Just as tragic is the influence of popular culture and perceptions causing youth to think the church powerless to speak against negative forces in our society. To do effective youth and family ministries, the church, like no other institution, is challenged to prepare leaders who bring power and hope to live outside the jar.

Effective youth ministry seeks to prepare faithful leaders and parents to produce a healthy church and society that will prepare youth with informed faith, vision, identity, and courage. This is the partnership we today call youth and family ministry. Its primary challenge is to reclaim the mission and vision of the church in the midst of a world where far too many youth experience the confines of the jar.

Tragically, more often than the church is willing to admit, one of the greatest confinements for youth begins within their own homes. Thus, there is tremendous danger in hanging the whole hat of the church around the popular mythology of "family" ministry. For far too many youth, the popular promotion of the family as an ideal confines them to their own jars—families or situations that don't fit this ideal. Rather, the church must recognize the family today as a vulnerable and imperfect institution that needs its support. To do so, the church has to expand its vision of the family to include many configurations as well as the nurturing network of parents, relatives, pastors, teachers, and caring adults who serve to inspire youth and offer them hope and direction.

The church also will need to understand youth and family ministry as organic to the total ministry and mission of the church. The church must be a source of power in contrast to the powerlessness youth feel in the presence of violence, drug and alcohol abuse, eating disorders, and consumerism. In its weekly worship, relationship building, programming, gathering in small groups, community associations, and parenting support, the church can offer to youth a clear model for the wholeness of God's embrace. In the example of worship, the church should provide a clear, strongly worded statement against racism, sexism, and homophobia. Each week, in neighborhoods and communities around the world, the church is called by God to extend God's invitation to gather and belong through worship. It does not matter who we are, where we come from, or what our age; congregational worship is to be a shared experience in which all feel welcome and needed.

One model of how the church has reshaped its response to youth and family ministries comes from Peer Ministry in Portland, Oregon. Peer Ministry was a collaboration between congregations and community to form a nurturing network for area youth. Congregation and community volunteers touched the lives of youth through activities such as sewing club, open gym at the local high school, overnights at churches, introductions to formal dining, youth forums, and trips and retreats to places like Holden Village Retreat Center and Disneyland.

Another example is provided by a youth I knew as D. During a weekend outing to a congregation in Port Angeles, Washington, D leaned over to me from the back seat of the van and whispered into my ear, "I had a really good time. Thanks for taking me on the retreat." His comment caught me off guard. I was tired and feeling sorry for myself for having missed the sacred Michigan-Notre Dame football game and much-needed sleep. D's comment called me to remember the reality of the youth with whom I was blessed to be. For them the retreat was an encounter with the powerful reality of the church as family (nurturing networks). Very simply, the retreat allowed them to be safe and healthy kids again, to experience life outside the jar.

Another example of the church functioning as a nurturing network leading youth through wilderness experiences came out of Holden Village, a Lutheran retreat center in the Cascade Mountain range near Chelan, Washington. Twice a year Holden Village became a nurturing network to a group of urban youth from Portland, Oregon. During their time at Holden, youth spent hours at the snack bar, in the game room and hot tub, hiking, and volunteering in the kitchen with adults. Among the many highlights for the youth was the experience of evening worship. The youth loved the evening vesper worship shared with the Holden staff and caring adult volunteers with whom they had formed meaningful relationships. One eleven-year-old youth, after spending hours in the craft room, emerged wearing around his neck what appeared to be a belt he had woven. He proudly corrected his peers, stating it was not a belt he had produced; rather, it was a stole. He stated that when he grows up he wants to be a pastor, like the one who brought him on the retreat. Today's youth need safe and supportive settings, much like the family settings many of us grew up in, where they will envision making a difference in the world when they grow up.

In the experience of youth today it is important to expand our understanding of the family to include those nurturing networks that support social, spiritual, and emotional development. Embracing families as nurturing networks celebrates two-parent nuclear families, single-parent families, and foster families as well as the role of grandparents, youth advisors, teachers, clergy, and coaches. It is said, "Time is the established currency of the millenium." Congregations can offer this wealth (time) as currency to invest in families, schools, and communities to support today's youth. Today the church is in the unique position to bring together a caring network of adults to nurture and offer hope to youth. Encourage youth to spend time, quality time, participating in worship and the life of the congregation. Encourage parents, grandparents, and single and elderly congregation members to participate in school and community activities. Effective youth and family ministry is a dynamic, powerful, and relation-centered enterprise. Youth and family ministry is the first step on the pathway for healthy congregations, schools, and communities.

Suggested Strategies

Caring Conversations. Ask your youth and families to identify the religious, educational, and civic institutions of which they are a part (for example, school, church, Rotary Club, YM/WCA, and so forth). How do these organizations create a healthy ecosystem or nurturing network for children, youth, and families? What are they missing? Who is or may feel excluded? What role can you play in strengthening and supporting these institutions?

Ritual or Tradition. Advertise every week the nurturing network of which your congregation and families are a part. Put out a display table featuring a different "network partner" each month. Invite speakers from these networks to address your congregation. Put information about these support systems in your bulletin and newsletters and on bulletin boards.

Family/Youth Group Devotion. The Bible is full of stories in which God works through community and government leaders to nurture the people. Check out these passages and identify the nurturing networks: Joseph as agriculture secretary and family reuniter (Genesis 41—45:15); Jonah as hesitant prophet and community renewer (read the whole book); Cyrus of Persia as liberator of the Israelites (Isaiah 45:1-6). Discuss how God used these people for "holy-istic" purposes and how God might use similar people today.

Servant/Retreat Event. Connect with the Search Institute and do an assets inventory of your youth and community. Complete the Search Institute's assets survey with your youth and families. Search Institute can help your congregation create nurturing networks. (For survey and other information, write or call Search Institute, 700 South Third Street, Suite 210, Minneapolis, MN 55415-1138; 1-800-888-7828.)

ENDNOTES

Preface

1. Loren B. Mead, *The Once and Future Church: Reinventing the Congregation for a New Mission Frontier* (New York: The Alban Institute, 1991), v.

2. Richard P. Olson and Joe H. Leonard, *A New Day for Family Ministry* (New York: The Alban Institute, 1996), 25-26.

3. Ibid., 54.

4. Based on an article first published in *Introductory Level Leadership Manual: Congregations and Families as Partners in Nurturing the Faith* copyright © 1997 Youth and Family Institute of Augsburg College. Adapted and reprinted by permission.

Proverb 2

1. See Mark H. Senter, *The Coming Revolution in Youth Ministry* (Colorado Springs, Colorado: Scripture Press Publications, 1992).

Proverb 3

1. Irene Goldenberg and Herbert Goldenberg, *Family Therapy: An Overview* (Pacific Grove, California: Brooks/Cole Publishing, 1980), 3.

2. Edwin H. Friedman, *Generation to Generation: Family Process in Church and Synagogue* (New York: Guilford Press, 1985), 19.

3. Rhonda R. Hanisch and Anne Marie Nuechterlein, "Our Mission and Ministry: Differentiated and Connected Identity and Relationships," *Pastoral Psychology* 38, no. 4 (Summer 1990): 205-12.

4. This proverb has been adapted from portions of Chapter 4 of the author's *Families of Alcoholics*.

Proverb 4

1. Mark DeVries, *Family-Based Youth Ministry: Reaching the Been-There, Done-That Generation* (Downers Grove, Illinois: InterVarsity Press, 1994), 37.

Proverb 5

1. Robert Sylwester, *A Celebration of Neurons: An Educator's Guide to the Human Brain.* (Alexandria, Virginia: Association for Supervision and Curriculum Development, 1995).

Proverb 7

1. Gerhard Kittel and Gerhard Friedrich, editors, *Theological Dictionary of the New Testament,* translated by Geoffrey W. Bromiley (Grand Rapids, Michigan: William B. Eerdmans Publishing Company, 1985), 2:517ff.

2. Ibid., 2:522.

3. Ibid., 2:531.

Proverb 9

1. See Annie Dillard, "An Expedition to the Pole," *Teaching a Stone to Talk* (New York: Harper and Row, 1982), 40-41.

Proverb 13

1. See Hillary Rodman Clinton, *It Takes a Village* (New York: Simon & Schuster, 1996). The author devotes a chapter to the importance of religion, relating how a youth minister opened her to issues of race and injustice and provided opportunities for her to learn to serve.

2. See James Whitehead and Evelyn E. Whitehead, *The Promise of Partnership: A Model for Collaborative Ministry* (San Francisco: Harper San Francisco, 1991).

Proverb 14

1. Martin Haendschke, *The Sunday School Story* (River Forest, Illinois: Lutheran Education Association, 1963), 3.

2. Ibid., 3.

3. Dr. Rollie Martinson of Luther Seminary draws this conclusion from his study of the Search Institute surveys.

4. Urie Bronfenbrenner, et. al., *The State of Americans* (New York: The Free Press, 1996), 2.

5. Search Institute, 700 S. Third Street, Suite 210, Minneapolis, MN 55415-1138

Proverb 15

1. Kennon L. Callahan, *Effective Church Leadership: Building on the Twelve Keys* (San Francisco: Jossey-Bass, Inc., 1997).

THE "I HAVE A QUESTION" INDEX

1. We are just getting started in youth and family ministry. How should we proceed?
Begin by establishing a study group that will read this book and discuss its implications. Move ahead after you are sure you are thinking in helpful ways and have identified the paradigm and assumptions under which you will operate (Proverb 14). Take time to state a clear vision for what you want to do (Proverb 1).

Begin a long-range planning process (Proverb 15 and Appendixes A and B) even as you pilot some of the ideas in this book. Be aware that it takes between three to five years to launch an effective youth and family ministry.

2. How can we involve more parents?
Introduce them to the Four Keys (preface and introduction). Select a few families to begin doing the Four Key activities in their home. Put Four Key activity suggestions in every Sunday bulletin for families to try in the coming week. Share Proverbs 3, 4, and 5 with parents, and help them understand the vital role they play in the faith formation of their child.

3. Our church is not very friendly when it comes to youth. What do you suggest?
Share Proverbs 2, 12, and 13. Review the promises we make in the baptismal liturgy of *Lutheran Book of Worship* with the congregational leaders.

4. We need more volunteers; how do we get them?
Emphasize Proverbs 2 and 4. Help volunteers see that all they need to be is authentic and available to young people. The Spirit will work through this relationship.

5. All our youth group does is activities. How can we deepen the experience?
Review Proverbs 1, 6, 7, 9, 16, and 17. Develop the W.O.L.F. Plan some devotional/Bible study events and go with whoever shows up!

6. We need to expand our understanding of church beyond the congregation "God Box." Any suggestions?
Review the preface and introduction, as well as Proverbs 4, 8, 14, 20, and 21.

7. How do we deal with disruptive youth?
Involve parents. Work on a three-to-one ratio of youth to adults. Review Proverbs 4, 8, 10, 17, 18, 19, and 21.

8. Our Christian education is often boring and academic. How can we teach the content in more interesting ways?
Review Proverbs 4, 8, 10, 13, 17, and 20.

9. We want to reach out to the unchurched youth in our neighborhood...how?
Proverbs 4, 8, 10, 11, 18, 19, and 21 can be of help. Most importantly, ask the right question. It is not, "How do we get them to come to church?" It is, "How do we connect with them in their world?"

10. It feels awkward to pray and do devotions. Help!
Check out Proverbs 7 and 9 and all the "Family/Youth Group Devotion" ideas at the end of each proverb.

11. We want to equip our youth for peer ministry. Any helps?
Read Proverb 19 and make sure you connect with the Youth and Family Institute of Augsburg College (Campus Box 70, 2211 Riverside Avenue, Minneapolis, MN 55454-1351; 612-330-1624).

12. I feel overwhelmed. Help!
Jesus builds the kingdom one person at a time. He was a small-group leader of 12. Start small, do pilots, and build relationships slowly. Youth and family ministry is an art form. Many successful people dealt with defeats and rejections time and again before their work bore fruit. Give yourself time, and pray for your youth and families. Remember your vision, paddle hard, and keep focused on your goal. The Spirit will bless your work.

13. Where can we go for further help?
Center for Youth Ministries, 333 Wartburg Place, Dubuque, Iowa 52005-5004; 319-589-0220; E-Mail: CYM@Ecunet.Org; Fax: 319-589-0333

Youth and Family Institute of Augsburg College, Campus Box 70, 2211 Riverside Avenue Minneapolis, MN 55454-1351; 612-330-1624

Youth Leadership, 122 West Franklin Avenue, Suite 510, Minneapolis, MN 55404; 612-870-4656

ELCA Youth Ministry Offices, 8765 West Higgins Road, Chicago, IL 60631; 1-800-NET-ELCA

Or contact any of our writers!

APPENDIX A
Identifying Your Current Strengths Relating to the 21 Proverbs

Attention, all youth and family ministers! Let's find out how you are doing paddling against the swift current. After reviewing a specific proverb, ask yourself, "Where does this proverb take shape in our congregation, and how do we support it happening in the home?" You will be surprised at how much you are already doing.

To do this, prepare a sheet for the proverb you are ready to evaluate. On the sheet first identify things you can currently celebrate (C). Then identify things that need only some tweaking (T) to be in line with the teachings of the proverb. Finally, identify things that you would like to add (A).

For an easy visual review, write your C's (celebrate) in green...they are a go! Write your T's (tweaks) in blue...cool and getting warmer. Write your A's (add) in red...as in, red alert.

Example:

The Gospel Proverb

How does this proverb take shape in our congregation?	How do we support this proverb happening in the home?
C Preaching from the pulpit	**T** Mail monthly Bible reading list
C Sunday school for all ages	**A** Family letters about each quarter's stories and themes

APPENDIX B
Long-Range Plan Guide

Follow this outline as you design your youth and family ministry future. It is important that you TAKE THESE STEPS IN ORDER. Your visioning team would be a good choice of people to do this planning.

Step 1: Prayer and reflection

Take some time in prayer to think about the mission of Jesus Christ (see Proverbs 1, 7, 9) and the place of Jesus in your life and the life of the church. Vision team and/or planning team members could be asked to do some journaling in this regard. Allow for some time to share what people have written in their journals.

Step 2: Paradigm shifts

What are the changes taking place around us, and which of our assumptions do these changes call into question? (Read the preface, introduction, and Proverb 14.)

Example A: We assume that the congregation is where faith is shaped. We now know that the home is the primary place of faith formation (see introduction). Therefore, what are we doing to help faith conversation take place in the home?

Example B: We assume that worship is best held on Sunday morning. Many of us in youth ministry suspect that teens are much more open to worship if it is held at 10:00 on Friday night in a nonchurch setting. What are we doing to offer a variety of worship settings, times, styles, and places?

Pray and reflect.

Step 3: Where are we going?

If you were to do nothing different from what you are doing right now, what are the logical consequences?

Pray and reflect.

Step 4: What do we hope the future holds?

Do you like the answer to step #3? Is there a future in this answer? Why or why not?

Pray and reflect.

Step 5: Who is it that we are trying to serve?

Can you identify a specific constituency or group of people that you are trying to serve? To say we welcome all may mean we are not intentional in our outreach. What are the people you wish to serve like? What are their needs, concerns, dreams, life situations, aspirations? Is there a group that you have overlooked?

Example: Many a congregation is located near a public school and has made no attempt to connect with that school. After-school tutoring, mentoring programs, safe centers, child-care programs, and parenting classes for pregnant teens are only some of the options to consider.

Pray and reflect.

Step 6: Where do we want to grow to?

Having identified possible youth ministries, are there places you want to be and things you want to do?

Pray and reflect.

Step 7: What are our assets, talents, and resources?

Review the work done in Appendix A. In particular, look at your "C's" and "T's." Rather than focus on our needs and weaknesses, we should ask, "What and who do we have going for us that we can utilize for a growing youth ministry future?"

Example: Brainstorm a list of all the assets you have. This list could include the following: a building, location, solid pastoral staff, parent volunteers, caring pool of senior citizens, and so forth.

Critical to this question is the issue of control. Are you willing to give up control and let the Spirit guide you? Can you allow for all these gifts and competencies to shape ministry in ways that may not be anticipated? Those who need to control all youth ministry are a hindrance to the Spirit. The key to giving up control without moving into chaos is the appreciation that the vision statement guides all decisions and shapes the character of the ministry!

Pray and reflect.

Step 8: What is God's mission for us?

What does God want you to do? The insights of the visioning team are very helpful at this time. Are there Biblical passages that can be guides for you? For example, Matthew 28:19 does not read, "Go therefore to the edges of the parking lot and make disciples...." Are you thinking big enough?

Pray and reflect.

Step 9: What is our vision?

Put into a concise statement what you have concluded from step #8. A vision statement is very general and broad and should inspire. It should be easily memorized.

Example A: The vision statement for Wartburg Theological Seminary is "Where learning leads to mission." That's it! Though short, it motivates and moves an entire seminary.

Example B: The vision statement of the Center for Youth Ministries of Wartburg Seminary is "We educate, advocate for, and inspire leaders in Christ's ministry by, with, and for youth." Our entire program runs on the energy of these few words.

Pray and reflect.

Step 10: What is our specific mission?

It's time to focus the planning process. In one or two paragraphs, can you focus your vision to a specific mission in this specific context? The mission statement of Wartburg Seminary is a full page, single-spaced (I still think it is too long). However, it gives specific grounding for the driving vision of the seminary.

Pray and reflect.

Step 11: What is unique about what we are doing?

Are you clear that you are not duplicating a ministry that is already taking place? Have you checked your ecumenical lines to see if there are ways you can do youth and family ministry cooperatively?

Pray and reflect.

Step 12: What are our goals?

It is best to review Proverb 15 for the full details on how to do this.

Pray and reflect.

Step 13: What strategies can we use to meet these goals?

See Proverb 17.

Pray and reflect.

Step 14: What staff/people resources do we need to meet these goals?

Many churches ask this question too soon. There is a tendency to seek staff and hire them to do the work. This is usually a prescription for failure. Questions of staffing come very late in the process so that when/if someone is hired to facilitate youth and family ministry, the necessary skills are most effectively identified and utilized. Effective youth and family ministers serve more as volunteer coordinators than "do it all" types.

Pray and reflect.

Step 15: What kinds of facilities will help us meet our goals?

Facilities will dictate your youth and family ministry program. Space shapes program. Consider these truths before a single nail is pounded or brick laid. It is tragic in this time of intergenerational contact and learning that Sunday school buildings are being created that continue to segregate children by ages. Permanent walls are permanent; barriers are not what you desire. Facility designs need to be flexible; the less that you build that cannot change, move, and be adapted, the better.

Consider this thought: If primary faith formation takes place in the home, perhaps the best place to do youth and family ministry is not in the "God Box" at all. If you need to expand ministry, think about involving more home sites or renting non–God Box facilities that may be more inviting to those you wish to reach.

Pray and reflect.

Step 16: Where is our mission money (budget)?

Only after considering all the previous steps should you consider the costs. See Proverb 17 for the reason. In considering costs make sure you have thought about ongoing expenses as well as initial start-up costs. How are you going to sustain your youth and family ministry program?

Pray and reflect.

Step 17: What is our time line?

What can you do in the next 30 days? The next three months? The next six months, and the first year? Identify these tasks and put a date on when they will be completed. Make sure that you know who is going to complete these tasks.

Pray and reflect.

Step 18: How will we continue to review our plans?

Evaluate your youth and family ministry activities. Seek feedback from all participants. Use evaluation forms that can be collated. At least once a year the vision/planning team should update the plan and adjust it for God's future mission.

APPENDIX C
Sample Youth and Family Ministry Job Description

(Thanks to Certification School number nine
of the Center for Youth Ministries of Wartburg Seminary.)

VISION
A youth and family ministry leader shares the vision of creating a faith-forming Christian community.

MISSION
Her or his mission is to partner home and congregation in ministry to establish personal trusted relationships, while sharing and participating in the gospel story, utilizing the Four Keys approach, and incorporating the 21 proverbs.

GOAL
His or her goal is to establish a holistic approach to youth and family ministry.

STRATEGY POSSIBILITIES
a. Study *Up the Creek WITH a Paddle* to shape this holistic approach.
b. Consider using these resources as part of your programming: *Parent Conversations* (Creative Confirmation series); *Back and Forth* (Living in Grace series); the intergenerational piece from *Family Life* (YouthTalk series). Contact Augsburg Fortress for materials.
c. Host a "Hand in Hand: Partnering Home and Congregation" seminar. Contact the Center for Youth Ministries of Wartburg Seminary for help.
d. Become a "Child in Our Hands" teaching congregation. Contact the Center for Youth Ministries of Wartburg Seminary or the Youth and Family Institute of Augsburg College in Minneapolis, Minnesota, for help.

GIFTS and QUALIFICATIONS NECESSARY TO BE A YOUTH AND FAMILY MINISTER
a. A deep sense of Christian spiritual journey or pilgrimage.
b. Ability to relate to people of all ages.
c. Demonstrated ability to love kids and love God.
d. Listening skills especially tuned to hear personal/family and corporate faith stories.
e. Ability to articulate a youth and family ministry vision that is guided by the biblical witness, the confessional heritage, the church historical record, and current research.
f. Ability to disciple/coach/teach/mentor others.
g. A flexible ministry style.
h. Ability to celebrate his or her own and others' experiences of God.
i. Knowledge of Scripture.
j. Ability to plan, organize, and administer efficiently.
k. Ability to design and implement intergenerational events.
l. Knowledge of child and youth development and family dynamics.
m. A strong personal moral ethic and the ability to establish appropriate boundaries.
n. Ability to establish a safe environment.
o. Ability to discern sound theological and educational materials.
p. Oral and written communication skills.
q. Ability to establish age-appropriate ministries.
r. Ability to implement financial support strategies, including budgeting and fund-raising.

WILLINGNESS FACTORS
a. Willing to take risks, pilot, and experiment.
b. Willing to see the Spirit unleash power, rather than control the process.
c. Willing to do ministry away from the congregation "God Box."
d. Willing to be a team player.
e. Willing to support, affirm, and encourage others.
f. Willing to share her or his own faith experiences.
g. Willing to ask for help.
h. Willing to claim his or her authority and role.
i. Willing to network.
j. Willing to delegate and coach.
k. Willing to nurture parents to be evangelists to their own children.
l. Willing to evaluate ministries and be accountable to the leadership within the congregation.
m. Willing to give God and others credit.
n. Willing to paddle hard.

SALARY GUIDELINE
We suggest a new youth worker's salary be roughly the equivalent of a beginning teacher's salary in your area.

Up the Creek WITH a Paddle: Building Effective Youth and Family Ministry © 1998, 1999 Augsburg Fortress. May be reproduced for local use.

ABOUT THE AUTHORS

Dr. David Anderson is the codeveloper of the "Child in Our Hands" initiative and the "Hand in Hand: Partnering Home and Congregation" seminar series. He is an internationally known speaker and teacher in family ministry. A parent and former parish pastor, Dr. Anderson now serves as adjunct faculty with the Center for Youth Ministries of Wartburg Seminary and is on the staff of the Youth and Family Institute of Augsburg College in Minneapolis, Minnesota.

Rev. Paul Hill is the developer and director of the Center for Youth Ministries of Wartburg Seminary in Dubuque, Iowa. He has nearly 30 years experience in youth ministry and is a parent, former parish pastor, and certified camp director and adventure education facilitator. Hill is a specialist in providing continuing education opportunities relating to youth and family ministry. With Dr. Anderson he has developed the "Hand in Hand: Partnering Home and Congregation" seminar series.

Rev. Mike Rinehart is pastor at Grace Lutheran Church in Conway, Texas. He has served as associate pastor in Charleston, North Carolina, and Davenport, Iowa. He serves on the advisory board to the Center for Youth Ministries of Wartburg Seminary. He is a musician, writer, pastor, youth ministry innovator, and parent.

Dr. Anne Marie Nuechterlein teaches courses in pastoral care and spirituality at Duke Divinity School in Durham, North Carolina, and is a psychotherapist in private practice. Her doctoral degree is in marriage and family counseling. She served on the faculty as Professor of Contextual Education at Wartburg Seminary. She is a parent and has ministered as a pastor, campus pastor, and pastoral therapist. She is author of *Improving Your Multiple Staff Ministry* and *Families of Alcoholics,* and coauthor of *The Male/Female Church.*

Dr. Susan K. Sherwood is Associate Professor of Education at Wartburg College in Waverly, Iowa. She was a first-grade teacher for 19 years, taught preschool summer school, and is a parent. Her doctoral degree is from the University of Northern Iowa, in curriculum and instruction. Her related field of study is early childhood education.

Dr. Ralph Quere is Professor of History and Theology at Wartburg Theological Seminary in Dubuque, Iowa. He is author of *Evangelical Witness* and codeveloper of the rock gospels "Most Excellent Theophilus" and "Prodigal." He has a lifelong passion and commitment to evangelism and has served as a parish pastor. He is a parent and a member of the executive committee of the Center for Youth Ministries of Wartburg Seminary.

Dr. Thomas Schattauer is Associate Professor of Liturgics and Dean of the Chapel at Wartburg Seminary. He previously taught at the Divinity School and Institute of Sacred Music at Yale University. His recent publications concern issues surrounding the relation of worship to contemporary North American culture, as well as the liturgical work of the nineteenth-century German pastor Wilhelm Loehe. Dr. Schauttauer is also a parent.

Rev. Elizabeth C. Polanzke is a parish pastor at St. John Evangelical Lutheran Church in Capac, Michigan. She is a specialist in young adult ministry and has done extensive work in the area of generational studies. She is a former student assistant to the Center for Youth Ministries of Wartburg Seminary and was a tremendous help in organizing this book.

Dr. Winston Persaud is Professor of Systematic Theology at Wartburg Theological Seminary in Dubuque, Iowa. He is from Guyana, South America, and has served as a parish pastor in Guyana. He has provided key leadership in the area of youth ministry in Guyana and through his work with the Center for Youth Ministries. Dr. Persaud is also a parent.

Rev. JoAnn A. Post has served Lutheran congregations in Alaska, Georgia, and Wisconsin. As a parish pastor she has had extensive experience with youth and campus ministries. She is also a parent.

Dr. Norma Cook Everist is Professor of Church Administration and Educational Ministry at Wartburg Theological Seminary in Dubuque, Iowa. She is author of many books, including the recently published *Where in the World Are You?* (Alban Press). She writes monthly for *The Lutheran* magazine and is an internationally known speaker and teacher and a parent.

Ms. Janet Lepp is a professional music educator who has worked with youth as a band director, choir director, and piano instructor. She is the developer and director of the Holy Trinity Lutheran Choir School in Dubuque, Iowa, where she works directly with involving youth in congregational worship. She also is an associate instructor and coach for the Center for Youth Ministries of Wartburg Seminary and a certified youth worker. She is also a parent.

Rev. Anne Helmke has served as a parish pastor and is a gang summit organizer and facilitator. Her efforts in addressing gang violence have been recognized by the San Antonio Bar Association. She is a student at the Gandhi Institute for Nonviolence. She is the animating director of a new Peace Center in San Antonio, Texas, and a member of the advisory board for the Center for Youth Ministries of Wartburg Seminary. She is also a parent.

Lyle M. Griner has been in youth and family ministry for more than 20 years and is now national director of Peer Ministry, a branch of the Youth and Family Institute of Augsburg College. He is also a parent. His favorite quote is from an unknown sage: "Anyone can count the seeds in an apple, but no one can count the apples in a seed."

Rev. Ralph Yernberg is executive director of Crossways Outdoor Ministries in northern Wisconsin and has served as a camp director in Minnesota. He is the author of *The History of Outdoor Ministries of the Lutheran Church* and has written countless curriculums and articles for outdoor ministries of the Evangelical Lutheran Church in America. He is a parent and is widely known for his creative youth programming skills.

Rev. Kelly Chatman is the national director for youth ministries of the Evangelical Lutheran Church in America. He has 20 years of experience in working with youth of a variety of backgrounds and settings. He was the Volunteer of the Year for the Portland Public Schools and Citizen of the Year for the city of Portland, Oregon, where he served a parish.